D1487168

ALL

the collected

short poems

1923 - 1964

ALL

the collected

short poems

1923-1964

Louis Zukofsky

The Norton Library
W · W · NORTON & COMPANY · INC · NEW YORK

W. W. Norton & Company, Inc., also publishes *The Norton Anthology of English Literature*, edited by M. H. Abrams et al; *The Norton Anthology of Poetry*, edited by Arthur M. Eastman et al; *World Masterpieces*, edited by Maynard Mack et al; *The Norton Reader*, edited by Arthur M. Eastman et al; *The Norton Facsimile of the First Folio of Shakespeare*, prepared by Charlton Hinman; *The Norton Anthology of Modern Poetry*, edited by Richard Ellmann and Robert O'Clair; *The Norton Anthology of Short Fiction*, edited by R. V. Cassill; *The Norton Anthology of American Literature*, edited by Ronald Gottesman et al; and the *Norton Critical Editions*.

SBN 393 00621 2

PRINTED IN THE UNITED STATES OF AMERICA

3 4 5 6 7 8 9 0

to
Paul

Contents

55 Poems

اسرار جهان چنانکه در دفتر ماست

گفتن نتوان که آن وبال سر ماست

چون نیست درین مردم دانا اهلی

نتوان گفتن مرا آنچه در خاطر ماست

عمر خیام

Poem beginning "The"

Because I have had occasion to remember, quote, paraphrase, I dedicate this poem to Anyone and Anything I have unjustifiably forgotten. Also to J. S. Bach—309,* Bede's *Ecclesiastical History* —248, 291, Max Beerbohm—245, Beethoven's *Ninth Symphony*— 310–312, Broadway—134, Geoffrey Chaucer—1st Movement, Title, College Cheer—45, E. E. Cummings' *Is Five*—38, Dante— 66, Norman Douglas' *South Wind*—14, Elijah, the Prophet—24, T. S. Eliot's *The Waste Land* and *The Sacred Wood*—25–27, John Erskine—184, 185, Heinrich Heine—266, 267, 269, 316, Robert Herrick—187, 188, Horace—141, Horses—224–237, Aldous Huxley's *Those Barren Leaves*—12, 18, Henry James— 2nd Movement, Title, Jewish Folk Song—191, 270–280, James Joyce—13, 20, 28, 29, D. H. Lawrence—8, 19, 133, Christopher Marlowe's *Edward II*—46, 47, Modern Advertising—163, George Moore—24, Marianne Moore—22, Mussolini—74, 75, Myself— 130, 142, 167, 309, Obvious—Where the Reference is Obvious, Walter Pater's *Renaissance*—165, *Peer Gynt*—281–285, Poe's *Helen*—168–182, Popular Non-Sacred Song—4, 5, 36, 37, 288, 289, Ezra Pound—15, 18, Power of the Past, Present, and Future— Where the reference is to the word Sun, E. A. Robinson's *Children of the Night*—132, Sophocles—6, Oswald Spengler—132, Max Stirner—199–202, Symbol of our Relatively Most Permanent Self, Origin and Destiny—Wherever the reference is to the word Mother, *The Bible*—1–3, 9, 313, 314, The Bolsheviki—203, 323, The French Language—31, 33, 51, 292, The King's English—166, *The Merchant of Venice*—250–265, The Yellow Menace—241– 242, University Extension—70, Villon—21, Franz Werfel—68, Virginia Woolf's *Mrs. Dalloway*—52, Yehoash—110–129, 205– 223, 318–330.

* References following dashes are to lines in *Poem beginning "The."*

Poem beginning "The"

1　The
2　Voice of Jesus I. Rush singing
3　　　　　　　　　in the wilderness
4　A boy's best friend is his mother,
5　It's your mother all the time.
6　Residue of Oedipus-faced wrecks
7　Creating out of the dead,—
8　From the candle flames of the souls of dead mothers
9　Vide the legend of thin Christ sending her
　　　　　out of the temple,—
10　Books from the stony heart, flames rapping
　　　　　the stone,
11　Residue of self-exiled men
12　By the Tyrrhenian.
13　　　　　　　　Paris.
14　But everywhere only the South Wind, the
　　　　　sirocco, the broken Earth-face.
15　The broken Earth-face, the age demands an
　　　　　image of its life and contacts,
16　Lord, lord, not that we pray, are sure of
　　　　　the question,
17　But why are our finest always dead?
18　And why, Lord, this time, is it Mauberly's
　　　　　Luini in porcelain, why is it Chelifer,
19　Why is it Lovat who killed Kangaroo,
20　Why Stephen Daedalus with the cane of
　　　　　ash,
21　But why les neiges?
22　And why, if all of Mary's Observations
　　　　　have been made
23　Have not the lambs become more sapient
　　　　　drinking of the spring;
24　Kerith is long dry, and the ravens that

              brought the prophet bread
25 Are dust in the waste land of a raven-
              winged evening.
26 And why if the waste land has been explored,
              traveled over, circumscribed,
27 Are there only wrathless skeletons exhumed
              new planted in its sacred wood,
28 Why—heir, long dead,—Odysseus, wandering of ten years
29 Out-journeyed only by our Stephen, bibbing
              of a day,
30 O why is that to Hecuba as Hecuba to he!
31 You are cra-a-zee on the subject of babies,
              says she,
32 That is because somehow our authors have been
              given a woman's intuition.
33 Il y a un peu trop de femme in this South Wind.
34 And on the cobblestones, bang, bang, bang,
              myself like the wheels—
35 The tram passes singing
36 O do you take this life as your lawful wife,
37   I do!
38 O the Time is 5
39   I do!
40 O the Time is 5
41   I do!
42 O do you take these friends as your loves
              to wive,
43 O the Time is 5
44   I do!

45 For it's the hoo-doos, the somethin' voo-doos
46 And not Kings onelie, but the wisest men
47 Graue Socrates, what says Marlowe?
48 For it was myself seemed held
49 Beating—beating—
50 Body trembling as over an hors d'oeuvres—
51
52 And the dream ending—Dalloway! Dalloway—
53 The blind portals opening, and I awoke!

54 Let me be
55 Not by art have we lived,

56 Not by graven images forbidden to us
57 Not by letters I fancy,
58 Do we dare say
59 With Spinoza grinding lenses, Rabbaisi,
60 After living on Cathedral Parkway?

SECOND MOVEMENT: *International Episode*

61 This is the aftermath
62 When Peter Out and I discuss the theatre.
63 Evenings, our constitutional.
64 We both strike matches, both in unison,
65   to light one pipe, my own.
66 'Tis, 'tis love, that makes the world go
               round and love is what I dream.
67 Peter is polite and I to me am almost as
               polite as Peter.
68 Somehow, in Germany, the Jew goat-song
               is unconvincing—
69   How the brain forms its visions think-
               ing incessantly of the things,
70 Not the old Greeks anymore,—
71   the things themselves a shadow world
               scarce shifting the incessant
               thought—
72 Time, time the goat were an offering,
73 Eh, what show do we see tonight, Peter?
74 "Il Duce: I feel God deeply."
75   Black shirts—black shirts—some power
               is so funereal.

76 Lion-heart, frate mio, and so on in two
               languages
77 the thing itself a shadow world.
78 Goldenrod
79 Of which he is a part,
80 Sod
81 He hurried over
82 Underfoot,
83 Make now
84 His testament of sun and sky
85 With clod

86   To root what shoot
87   It sends to run the sun,
88   The sun-sky blood.
89   My loves there is his mystery beyond
               your loves.
90   Uncanny are the stars,
91   His slimness was as evasive
92   And his grimness was not yours,

93   Do you walk slowly the halls of the heavens,
94   Or saying that you do, lion-hearted not ours,
95   Hours, days, months, past from us and gone,
96   Lion-heart not looked upon, walk with the
               stars.
97   Or have these like old men acknowledged
98   No kin but that grips of death,
99   Of being dying only to live on with them
100   Entirely theirs,
101   And so quickly grown old that we on earth like
               stems raised dark
102   Feel only the lull, heave, phosphor
               change, death, the
103   One follow, the other, the end?

104   Our candles have been buried beneath these
               waters,
105   Their lights are his,
106   Ship-houses on the waters he might have lived
               near.
107   Steady the red light and it makes no noise
               whatever.
108   Damn it! they have made capital of his flesh
               and bone.
109   What, in revenge, can dead flesh and bone
               make capital?
110   And his heart is dry
111   Like the teeth of a dead camel
112   But his eyes no longer blink
113   Not even as a blind dog's.

114   With the blue night shadows on the sand
115   May his kingdom return to him,

116 The Bedouin leap again on his *asilah*,
117 The expanse of heaven hang upon his shoulder
118 As an embroidered texture,
119 Behind him on his saddle sit the night
120 Sing into his ear:

121 Swifter than a tiger to his prey,
122 Lighter than the storm wind, dust or spray,
123 The Bedouin bears the Desert-Night,
124 Big his heart and young with life,
125 Younger yet his gay, wild wife
126   The Desert-Night.

127 Some new trappings for his steed,
128 All the stars in dowry his meed
129   From the Desert-Night.

130 I've changed my mind, Zukofsky,
131 How about some other show—
132 "The Queen of Roumania," "Tilbury,"
            "The West-Decline,"
133 "Hall's Mills," "The Happy Quetzal-
            coatl,"
134 "Near Ibsen," "Dancing with H. R. H.,"
            "Polly Wants a New Fur Coat,"
135 "The Post Office"—
136 Speaking of the post office, the following
            will handicap you for the position,
137   my dear Peter,
138 Your weight less than one hundred
            twenty-five pounds,
139 One half of a disabled veteran, and
            probably
140   the whole of an unknown soldier,
141 That's indomitaeque morti for you.

142 Is it true what you say, Zukofsky,
143 Sorry to say, My Peter Out.

144 "Tear the Codpiece Off, A Musical
            Comedy,"
145 Likewise, "Panting for Pants,"

THIRD MOVEMENT: *In Cat Minor*

147   Hard, hard the cat-world.
148   On the stream Vicissitude
149   Our milk flows lewd.

150   We'll cry, we'll cry,
151   We'll cry the more
152   And wet the floor,

153   Megrow, megrow,
154   Around around,
155   The only sound

156   The prowl, our prowl,
157   Of gentlemen cats
158   With paws like spats

159   Who weep the nights
160   Till the nights are gone—
161   —And r-r-run—the Sun!

FOURTH MOVEMENT: *More "Renaissance"*

162   Is it the sun you're looking for,
163   Drop in at Askforaclassic, Inc.,
164   Get yourself another century,
165   A little frost before sundown,
166   It's the times don'chewknow,
167   And if you're a Jewish boy, then be your
           Plato's Philo.

168   Engprof, thy lectures were to me
169   Like those roast flitches of red boar
170   That, smelling, one is like to see
171   Through windows where the steam's galore
172   Like our own "Cellar Door."

173   On weary bott'm long wont to sit,
174   Thy graying hair, thy beaming eyes,

175 Thy heavy jowl would make me fit
176   For the Pater that was Greece.
177   The siesta that was Rome.

178 Lo! from my present—say not—itch
179   How statue-like I see thee stand
180 Phi Beta Key within thy hand!
181   Professor—from the backseats which
182 Are no man's land!

183 Poe,
184 Gentlemen, don'chewknow,
185 But never wrote an epic.

FIFTH MOVEMENT: *Autobiography*

186 Speaking about epics, mother,
187 How long ago is it since you gathered
      mushrooms,
188 Gathered mushrooms while you mayed.
189 It is your mate, my father, boating.
190 A stove burns like a full moon in a desert night.
191 Un in hoyze is kalt. You think of a new
      grave,
192 In the fields, flowers.
193 Night on the bladed grass, bayonets dewed.
194 It is your mate, my father, boating.
195 Speaking about epics, mother,—
196 Down here among the gastanks, ruts,
      cemetery-tenements—
197 It is your Russia that is free.
198 And I here, can I say only—
199   "So then an egoist can never embrace
      a party
200   Or take up with a party?
201   Oh, yes, only he cannot let himself
202   Be embraced or taken up by the party."
203 It is your Russia that is free, mother.
204 Tell me, mother.

205 Winged wild geese, where lies the passage,
206 In far away lands lies the passage.

207 Winged wild geese, who knows the pathway?
208 Of the winds, asking, we shall say:
209 Wind of the South and wind of the North
210 Where has our sun gone forth?
211 Naked, twisted, scraggly branches,
212 And dark, gray patches through the branches,
213 Ducks with puffed-up, fluttering feathers
214 On a cobalt stream.
215 And faded grass that's slowly swaying.
216 A barefoot shepherd boy
217 Striding in the mire:
218 Swishing indifferently a peeled branch
219 On jaded sheep.
220 An old horse strewn with yellow leaves
221 By the edge of the meadow
222 Draws weakly with humid nostrils
223 The moisture of the clouds.
224 Horses that pass through inappreciable
         woodland,
225 Leaves in their manes tangled, mist, autumn
         green,
226 Lord, why not give these bright brutes—
         your good land—
227 Turf for their feet always, years for their mien.
228 See how each peer lifts his head, others follow,
229 Mate paired with mate, flanks coming full
         they crowd,
230 Reared in your sun, Lord, escaping each hollow
231 Where life-struck we stand, utter their praise
         aloud.
232 Very much Chance, Lord, as when you first
         made us,
233 You might forget them, Lord, preferring what
234 Being less lovely where sadly we fuss?
235 Weed out these horses as tho they were not?
236 Never alive in brute delicate trembling
237 Song to your sun, against autumn assembling.

238 If horses could but sing Bach, mother,—
239 Remember how I wished it once—
240 Now I kiss you who could never sing Bach,
         never read Shakespeare.

241 In Manhattan here the Chinamen are yellow
         in the face, mother,
242 Up and down, up and down our streets they
         go yellow in the face,
243 And why is it the representatives of your,
         my, race are always hankering for
         food, mother?
244 We, on the other hand, eat so little.
245 Dawn't you think Trawtsky rawthaw a
         darrling,
246 I ask our immigrant cousin querulously.
247 Naw! I think hay is awlmawst a Tchekoff.
248 But she has more color in her cheeks than
         the Angles—Angels—mother,—
249 They have enough, though. We should
         get some more color, mother.
250 If I am like them in the rest, I should
         resemble them in that, mother,
251 Assimilation is not hard,
252 And once the Faith's askew
253 I might as well look Shagetz just as much
         as Jew.
254 I'll read their Donne as mine,
255 And leopard in their spots
256 I'll do what says their Coleridge,
257 Twist red hot pokers into knots.
258 The villainy they teach me I will execute
259 And it shall go hard with them,
260 For I'll better the instruction,
261 Having learned, so to speak, in their
         colleges.
262   It is engendered in the eyes
263   With gazing fed, and fancy dies
264   In the cradle where it lies
265   In the cradle where it lies
266 I, Senora, am the Son of the Respected
         Rabbi,
267 Israel of Saragossa,
268 Not that the Rabbis give a damn,
269 Keine Kadish wird man sagen.

270 Under the cradle the white goat stands, mother,
271 What will the goat be saddled with, mother?
272   Almonds, raisins
273 What will my heart be bartering, mother,
274   Wisdom, learning.
275 Lullaby, lullaby, lullaby, lullaby.
276 These are the words of the prophet, mother,
277 Likely to save me from Tophet, mother—
278 What will my heart be burning to, mother,
279   Wisdom, learning.
280 By the cat and the well, I swear, my
          Shulamite!
281 In my faith, in my hope, and in my love.
282 I will cradle thee, I will watch thee,
283 Sleep and dream thou, dear my boy!
284   (Presses his cheek against her mouth.)
285 I must try to fare forth from here.
286 I do not forget you,
287 I am just gone out for to-night,
288 The Royal Stag is abroad,
289 I am gone out hunting,
290 The leaves have lit by the moon.
291 Even in their dirt, the Angles like Angels
          are fair,
292 Brooks Nash, for instance, faisant un petit
          bruit, mais très net,
293 Saying, He who is afraid to do that should
          be denied the privilege,
294 And where the automobile roads with the
          gasoline shine,
295 Appropriately the katydid—
296 Ka-ty did . . . . Ka-ty didn't . . . .

297 Helen Gentile,
298 And did one want me; no.
299 But wanted me to take one? yes.
300 And should I have kissed one? no.
301 That is, embraced one first
302 And holding closely one, then kissed one?
          yes.

303 Angry against things' iron I ring
304 Recalcitrant prod and kick.
305 Oh, Baedekera Schönberg, you here
306   dreaming of the relentlessness of motion
307 As usual,
308 One or two dead in the process what does it
            matter.

309 Our God immortal such Life as is our God,
310 Bei dein Zauber, by thy magic I embrace
            thee,
311 Open Sesame, Ali Baba, I, thy firefly, little
            errant star, call here,
312 By thy magic I embrace thee.

313 O my son Sun, my son, my son Sun!
            would God
314 I had died for thee, O Sun, my son, my
            son!

315 I have not forgotten you, mother,—
316 It is a lie—Aus meinen grossen leiden mach ich
            die kleinen lieder,
317 Rather they are joy, against nothingness joy—
318 By the wrack we shall sing our Sun-song
319 Under our feet will crawl
320 The shadows of dead worlds,
321 We shall open our arms wide,
322 Call out of pure might—
323 Sun, you great Sun, our Comrade,
324 From eternity to eternity we remain true to you,
325 A myriad years we have been,
326 Myriad upon myriad shall be.

327 How wide our arms are,
328 How strong,
329 A myriad years we have been,
330 Myriad upon myriad shall be.

1

Memory of V. I. Ulianov

Immemorial,
And after us
Immemorial,
O white
O orbit-trembling,
Star, thru all the leaves
Of elm;—
Lighted-one, beyond the trunk tip
Of the elm
High, proportionately vast,
Of mist and form;—
Star, of all live processes
Continual it seems to us,
Like elm leaves,
Lighted in your glow;—
We thrive in strange hegira
Here below,
Yet sometimes in our flight alone
We speak to you,
When nothing that was ours seems spent
And life consuming us seems permanent,
And flight of stirring beating up the night
And down and up; we do not sink with every wave.
Travels our consciousness
Deep in its egress.
Eclipsed the earth, for earth is power
And we of earth.
Eclipsed our death, for death is power
And we of death.
Single we are, tho others still may be with us
And we for others.
We have come to the sources of being,

Inviolable, throngs everlasting, rising forever,
Rush as of river courses,
Change within change of forces.
Irrevocable yet safe we go,
Irrevocable you, too,
O star, we speaking to you,
The shadows of the elm leaves faded,
Only the trunk of elm now dark and high
Unto your height:
Now and again you fall,
Blow dark and burn again,
And we in turn
Share now your fate
Whose process is continual.

2

Not much more than being,
Thoughts of isolate, beautiful
Being at evening, to expect
                    at a river-front:

A shaft dims
With a turning wheel;

Men work on a jetty
By a broken wagon;

Leopard, glowing-spotted,
      The summer river—
Under: The Dragon:

Cocktails
and signs of
"ads"

flashing,
light's waterfalls,

Bacchae
among electric lights

will swarm the crowds
streamers of the lighted

skyscrapers

nor tripping
over underbrush

but upon pavement

and not with thyrsus
shall they prick

the body of their loves
but waist to waist

laugh out in gyre—
announced then upon stairs,

not upon hills,
will be their flight

when passed turnstiles,
having dropped

coins
they've sprinted up

where on the air (elevated)
waves flash—and out—

leap
signaling—lights below

4

         Buoy—no, how,
It is not a question: what
Is this freighter carrying?—
Did smoke blow?—That whistle?—
Of course, commerce will not complete
Anything, yet the harbor traffic is busy,
                there shall be a complete fragment

Of—

Nothing, look! that gull
Streak the water!
Getting nearer are we,
Hear? count the dissonances,

Shoal? accost—cost
Cost accounting.

5

Ferry

Gleams, a green lamp
In the fog:
Murmur, in almost
A dialogue

Siren and signal
Siren to signal.

Parts the shore from the fog,
Rise there, tower on tower,
Signs of stray light
And of power.

Siren to signal
Siren to signal.

Hour-gongs and the green
Of the lamp.

Plash. Night. Plash. Sky.

6

How many
Times round

Deck, ladies?

What says
The nigger?

"Fi' minutes
After a

Man's breath
Leaves

His body
He knows—'

Much 'bout
Himself 's

Ten years
Befo' 'e

Was bo'n—"

What you
Say to

That, ladies?

The Statue
Of Liberty's

Drunk?!
French! !

7

During the Passaic Strike of 1926

the sexton of the rich parish of St. Mark's-on-the-Bouwerie, New York, imparted the news to my friend, S.T.H., that there was only room for two in his graveyard.

There are two vaults left in St. Mark's-on-the-Bouwerie,
There are two vaults left to bury the dead,
O when the two vaults are filled in St. Mark's-on-the-Bouwerie,
How will the dead bury their dead?

For Justice they are shrewdly killing the proletarian,
For Justice they are shrewdly shooting him dead,
Good Heavens, when the vaults are filled in St. Mark's-on-the-
        Bouwerie,
How will the dead bury their dead!

("I was born indeed in your dominions, but your service was hard, and your wages such as a man could not live on"—Pilgrim's Progress.)

8

And to paradise which is a port
And over water-trestle,
And as over a sea so over: and by the way
      of this train's movement

Water-staves,
Moorings, spread blue coats of water,
Long,
Along,
Long.

A dying away as of trees
       where a hill-street pavement
       is broken into rocks:

A car sounds,

       Climbs.
     Empty, late Saturday.

At the bottom of the grade
       stopped short in one's rounds
       this tree-dying night of hurrying towards Sunday,
          uptorn by an empty trolley's rumble on usual
                                pursuits,
         retreats to meet
         street after empty street,
         hills paved, rising to be climbed,
         and what for houses but for windows?
         sure forecast of ongrowing moonlight.

10

        Passing tall
        Who walk upon the green
        So light they are not heard
        If never seen;—

        Willow above in spring haze,
        Green sprig and pendulous;—
        Wind, white lightning
        In branches over us;

        Sun;
        All weathering changing loves,
        In the high grass (kiss!)
        Will not uncover us.

11

Stubbing the cloud-fields—the searchlight, high
In the roseate twilight of rain-sky, green! green spring
In the heavens mild in the spring; or down suddenly
Earthwards, plunge deep suddenly earthwards,
Like escape, stampede of cattle horns, ghastly, ghastly
Their giant heads invisible for joy, grief, cavalcade,
                                    plunge earthwards,
And into our hearts, O sacrifice,
But we emerge! (emerge upon a level roof that fronts
                                    the sky,
The skylight of your room to rear,)
So we can breathe, the rain air and the spring
Ours, till again it moves along the sky
Down or up, machine-rayed, powerful!

12

Millennium of sun—
Beast of the field,—
Kissing the beast upon both ears—

O who will pluck geranium
With smiles before this ass's face
And tie it to his cranium
To match the ass's grace!

13

We are crossing the bridge now.
I can feel it by the sound
The wheels make over the waters.
To-night we cannot see
From the windows. But there are lights
Of two shores. And if you open the door
The water-wind blows in the brume
Which covers us.

14

Only water—

We seek of the water
The water's love!

Shall we go again
Breast to water-breast,

Gather the fish-substance,
The shining fire,
The phosphor-subtlety?

We sing who were many in the South,
At each live river mouth
Sparse-lighted, carried along!

15

And looking to where shone Orion,
Wickson—"The miracle were done
If she were to bear my son.

"As to taste there's no dispute.
But who is he may taste?
These miles of beach—
Coarse grass and ocean waste—

"Where on them can I get,
Or from their green of stars,
Something like a cucumber?"

16

Aubade, 1925

Kick the blanket away,
The man of darkness has sweated enough!
One, two, three efforts, and he stands on his feet—
Chilled a little on the cold sands.

Day. Still he is blinking man,
But eyes open: he sees
The sea, little waves, waves of the morning pearl-gray!

Agh! running the wind!

But think with the head!
This is the state of man
To raise his ashes to the dawn.
Jump, away from the coast-guard house,
Across one, two, three—! Sand mounds,

And a swamp,
Crosses of wood, newspapers in coarse island grass,
Behind a hill to be as simple as the horses.

Who has seen, who can, and who will ever see?
No one about but flat island sand and flat blue sky and
       a few mounds
Behind which—the sea, its reverberations.
Whence, if ever, then, will come sympathy?
Surely not out of the sun, nor out of the sky,
Nor out of eternity of flat island sand a little lowly to
    the aspect of eternal morning.

          Orbed sun! great air! slow time!
          The man of darkness
          Is his own monument,
          Moving his return—

Bah-h! so much blanket again—
Tousled hair—sleep!

Swims!
Spewing and spewn on to the land!
          The sun is hot!

17

    Cars once steel and green, now old,
    Find their grave at Cedar Manor.
    They rust in a wind
    The sky alone can hold.

    For the wind
    Flows heavily thru the mind like cold,
    Drums in the ears
    Till one knows its being which soon is not.

18

Tall and singularly dark you pass among the breakers—
Companionship as of another world bordering on this;
To the intelligence fastened by the senses you are lost
In a world of sunlight where nothing is amiss:

For nothing but the sun is there and peace vital with the sun,
The heaviest changes shift through no feature more than a smile,
Currents spread, and are gone, and as the high waves appear,
You dive, in the calming are as lost awhile.

How in that while intelligence escapes from sense
And fear with hurled human might darkens upon bliss!
Till as again you stand above the waters
Fear turns to sleep as one who dreamt of falling, an abyss!

19

Run on, you still dead to the sound of a name:
Climb, white froth, as on stems of flowers;

Pass near the curve of the heavens.
Sunned your whiteness is of winter frost.

For you, froth, the surge of blue-sweeping autumn,
Run to the gate of the snowed winter tomb
Where none ask why the death nor for whom;

Where the sun, too, grows small and of winter—
Drifted fruit, rotten.—

20

Close your eyes,
                    the sun low—upon them

Sky grows down, one petal
Daisy petal, broad, luminous.
A wind that makes for blindness—
                    Sun

21

O sleep, the sky goes down behind the poplars,
I scrape the gravel with my shoes and toe
The ties:
The milky moon is in the clearing,
Only the power-plant hurries in winter.

22

Cactus rose-mauve and gray, twin overturned
              natural play-paniers
in a burnt little earthen pot, green mortuary
              of plainness.
Cactus minus the red bud flower,
and the same day
              nescience of treading knee deep in snow,
always mortmain the oblivion of her
              in the desert of my traces—
Hannah, "grace." Grace under the moon,
              on blue velvet cloth I placed the prickly plant.

Think of snow.
Know duration.
All once grafted hers go to her,
              the plants, too, unseen continuance.

23

Song Theme

*To the last movement of Beethoven's Quartet
in C Sharp Minor*

All my days—
And all my ways—
Met by hands—
And ringed with feet—
Into laurel-branch the hands
Are gone, into fertile soil the feet;
    So these praised ones that are fallen off
    Are a signal in the trees,
    Are a beacon in the sun,—

    Sun and death and stir, and death's
                  unlit love,—
All their days
And all their ways.

24

tam cari capitis

I

Unlovely you called yourself
And at once I felt I was never lovely:
I, who had few truths to go to
Found you doubting what I loved.

Now I make you lovely my own way.
Unmentioned were we certain
Of a greater, in small assurances
Others may find trivial:

The same in all weathers.

And not till there is an end to singing
Will you go,
As you have always gone, quiet.

But like your birds that wake in the night
To sleep again:

25

Like the oceans, or the leaves of fine Southern
        palm, we must appear numbered
                to you, like the tides

Reaching up to you, also as leaves, calm, night-green,
        arching under you,
        Moon. And, O moon,
As we travail to sleep we do not know whether, with your
        genius furthering us,
We should be counted as the cuspid waves of the seas, or
        as the souls of trees
Whose leaves we are, growing for you, the crowded
        summits stark, heavenly.

Ask of the sun
and it may tell you—

if it will come
if it has come

that afternoon
of afternoons

when you'll have ended
shaping a plaything

circus horse of glass
a mane of beads

since art's high effort
vying with the sun's heat

shadows small—
when rather like thick peasants

out of Brueghel
after working

you stretch out—
the sun among

the hayricks of Its fields
and artless find time.

Blue light is the night harbor-slip.
If a number are gold they make a crown for the shore.
If three rise vertically, as one nethermost, another
                    over that, another topping,
All as if reaching, the vessel is making headway.

The scarf-pins of night-outers are sometimes that way
And, God's sky! if the body of something deploys one
                    gold light for'ard,
And, shy, a smile, may it be named? another gold light
                                        as trailer,
The general 'it is after midnight' may be a marriage,
                    or a return from the month's ball.

            Masquerade, Mozart,
            Filigree—they used to—

        (We had such a nice time)

Red! look out for this island!

Blue! and it hurts the eyes, metallic-glass this
                    beacon-light, many-faceted

It is generally safer here because,
                    in the white-washed ceiling hulk,
                    not only sparse lights for the deck
                    but life-belts

Danger! The general effect of gray light in darkness
                    is a man-of-war

Red!

Out far again
Lights—a branch laid on the world—
Their intermittence—

(We look abroad openly)

28 & 29

Two Dedications

Tibor Serly

Red varnish
Warm flitch

Of cello,
They play

Scroll before
Them—Sound

Breaks the
Sunset!—Kiss

With wide
Eyes—With

Their music
The (no?)

Pit, weather
Of tears

Which plagues
Us—Bodies

Of waves
Whose crests

Spear air,
Here rolls

The sea—
Go chase

It—a
Salt pact

Ranged over
Bars—white

Ribs pervade
In constant

Measures the
Rounds—Its

Wet frosting,
A kiss

Opens nothing,
Bend head

No! lips
Not this

An assumed
Poise among

Crowds! Blue—
Withdraws sunset—

Tones sound—
Pluck—dissonant—

Stops sing
The welter

D.R.

Comrade D.R.—
His murals speak:
Executives of industry,

Rich stone heads
Conferring at tables,
We peasants and

Workers, our faces
Becoming us more
Than frescoes of saints,

Marshal to say:
We are the
Heads over industry.

Our children, (backs
Pretty as lady bugs,
Red upon gold

Soil) now humbled
On stumps, grow
Up on soil

Turning black thru
Our efforts—water,
Our biceps, unspared.

Our mates, their mothers,
Shall know them—
Unflattered by dynamos—

Controlled among wheels
And controlling the
Glancing of belts

Against pulleys, Holidays—
There'll be many—
Will find friends

Rangers among palm
Leaf and tiger
Paw.

       Sunday; the
Miner's lantern unlit,
Coal beneath sun.

29 SONGS

1

Madison, Wis.,
remembering the bloom of Monticello (1931)

No empty bed blues—
    between these walls
I can lie—
    your thigh, me—

"Keep in it deer,
    rabbits, pigeons"—
"the figure will be better
    placed in this,"—

"Form a couch of moss"—
    queer guy
Tom Jefferson—all daughters
    no son

Sure, if you wish
    we can
turn the small Alleghenies
    to upper Japan—

But if Mr. citizen
    sells apples
in New York by
    the sea

Maybe that's
    where we
should be—
    I'll die—

The heart all
　　a queen's
the brain
　　　Lenin's—

Empty Bed
　　Blues—"keep the
thorn constantly
　　　wed."

2

Immature Pebbles

An Imponderable is an article of make-believe which has become
axiomatic by force of settled habit. It can accordingly cease to be
an Imponderable by a course of unsettling habit.
　　　　　　　　　　　　　　　　—THORSTEIN VEBLEN

There are several robins here,
their legs among the triple buds—
the spring is yet too brisk
for water suds, (bathers' dirt):
instead, where the trees almost
into the water grow—below them
over the split moistened stones, ripples
make for? An observer's irrelevancy
　　　　　　　　　　　of April.
Following: May.

Should then this repeated objectless
of inconsequence, following and May
bring the expected to the accustomed
in this place,
the surprise will, it can be seen, not exceed
legs of young men and women
bathing in a lake—
summer's inaction colored hot—
blue and crimson of their shivering suits
among the trees, no less ironic than what male,
encaged mandrill's blue and crimson
secret parts?

Observer, then, come get one going,
before one's an accessory to these ways,
obliged to accept "imponderables"—
those axioms of settling habits
no less, no more, attractive than a lake's inclusions—
pebbles, young humans   .   .   .
In our day, impatience
handles such matters of photography
more pertinently from a train window.

3

Prop. LXI

*(The Strength of The Emotions—Ethica ordine
geometrico demonstrata: IV)*

Confute leaf-
Point's water with slight dropped sounds,—
Turn coat, cheat facts, say for the spring's bloom's fall
The tree's trunk has set the circling horn-branch
To cipher each drop—the eye—shot in the rain around.

So cheated well
Let the fallen bloom-wet clutter down, and into   .   .   .
And the heart (fact   .   .) holds nothing, desire is
No excess, the eye points each leaf
The brain desire, the rain (cheat.) recites their brief.

4

Train-Signal

With stars past troughs to sound
—thru thick twilight
—by the stumps of the trees
blasts near the faces of leaves
by a hair's breadth separated:

with but a proof to the leaves'
closeness: leaf over leaf's face
with a hair: and the cheek kissed
with the shredded space.

5

It's a gay li - ife

There's naw—thing
    lak po—ee try
it's a delicacy
    for   a horse:

Dere's na—thing
    lak pea-   nut-brittle
it's a delicacy
    for   the molars.

6

—"her soil's birth"

(Madison)

Virtue in that—
If fall of pods' spring-seed to earth,
    Sun, ferns rise at,
Together glassed themselves in green, girth
With the windfall of her soil's birth.

    Rays sent from glass
Sphering with its beamed fall the air
    Could not surpass—
Designed to meet opposed beams there—
The unsealing of the eyes bare.

    Explosions such
As these are not for eyes to prink:
    Pods' fall too much
Inevitable, each pod will sink
Its green into a glass we drink.—

    Spring's air! which keeps
The sharpest rays of sun askew—
    Over pods sweeps:
Flecks green her hands—like ferns' virtue
In the sun keeping their green true.

7

Who endure days like this
with me   the room's inference
foghorns' tuned discs amiss
dropped our wrists would be
seconds   impatience' stem
gestures' graft   arms difference
eyes' blue iris splicing them

8

Happier, happier, now
For whom in snowsleet barberries see;
          If not that, if not that, how
Are red berries for their windsleights free?
The glaze of mind, winter of eyes,
          Snow's berries, meet!
The Void of mind, the fall of thighs,
          Cold winds heat.

          Yellow flowers dead, green of leaves
Still green, look out of what eyes in love's Void?
          The close, the unseeing and unseen,
The glaze of sight snowsleet has destroyed.
Windblown, for all barberries not dead
          See with love's tear,—
The fall of thighs; love's discrete forehead
          Happier.

In Arizona
        (how many years in the mountains)
The small stumped bark of a tree
Looks up
        in the shape of an adored pup

The indians do not approach it
The round indian tents
           remain where they are
The tanned whites
        are never seen by it
And one can imagine its imploring eyes

The skies
        it seems to look up to
             blue
The same sun that warms the desert
Warms what one
        can imagine to be its ears.

10

Arizona

    arch animals'
    upearthed faces—
    dust of
    their red, wrinkled—

    higher than the oil wells
    are the rocks—
    the fluted cactus, its
    spiked needle locks,

    rasp shard in
    the blue air, blood boil
    into the unprofitable
    eiffel towers of oil

11

Home For Aged Bomb Throwers—U.S.S.R.

When is winter spring?
When, tho ice is not breaking,
One has what one does not expect
                to be taking

It is against the winds
It is against firm ice
But with the sun, that
                        falling asleep
Winter is spring

1/6 of the earth

12

Whatever makes this happening
            Is unheard
            To a third.

Two. Where two should
            Stand. One. One.
            With the sun. In a wood.

Tomorrow is unsought.
            No oasis of ivy to inurn
            Either foot or fern.

13

in that this happening
            is not unkind
it put to
            shame every kindness

mind, mouths, their words
            people, put sorrow
                        on
            its body

before sorrow it came
            and before every kindness,
happening for every sorrow
            before every kindness;

14

The sand: For the cigarette finished
on the beach the universal ash-tray:

or where the bacon grease is spilt:
Knowledge: smell is taken up

and off by the seas'
winds:

                        a ship's
funnel is seen from this house
and rain drenches a witness of departure:

love as the relaxation among breakers
a dog-carcass—its wet—a reminder:

Do not leave me
    before that convert surfeit
which if it ever leaves toward you—
    never to your misgiving—
        inexistent
comes first to me in another

That surfeit—other—which
    much less you do not look for, distraction
from this our being together
    never surfeit—the owned
devolving upon—owned—and neither owned—

That distraction which neither of us
    much less you, close, seeks—love
never prior to your patience
    asks that surfeit come upon me first—
unowned misgiving;

it is but a mouth's mumblings:
    no distraction coming
after love, convert
    of your patience—a mouth knowing;
close, its unowned owner.

16

Crickets'
thickets

light,
delight:

sleeper's eyes,
keeper's;

       Plies!
lightning

frightening
whom . . . ?

doom
nowhere . . .

where eyes . . .
air,

are crickets'
air

17

Imitation*

N.Y. 1932

In the imitation of Gothic
building   and a virgin
as Virgin   her recessed space
Her alcove   its "statue"   a quadrangle
stones considered built   imitation

within a court   a garden   bluebells
in New York City   imitation of
a chalet   set apart for meals
familiar to Americans if not the Swiss

this institution   by deliberateness   of engraving
THE ACADEMY OF THE HOLY CHILD
to which dedicated from up
the rich street hurries   promised   young
the academician and wholly child
all his attention religiously kept by vast
cubic contents of gas tank built on principles of
a steel erector set given him by his aunt
just off the boat from Pekin   coloration of sea
plate steel rectangles mirrored blue at the water-line
the gas tank walls   the same composition   same color

—Xavier   you know, or have not you heard
in China even comparatively recently
the physicians attending women of the upper
class never saw their patients but for
a hand extended from behind a screen
for the taking of their pulse   and so   depended
for the rest of the diagnoses upon a proxy
a small carved figure of a woman
sometimes of ivory upon which the patient indicated
the approximate location of her complaint

other Chinese ivories   tablets which were held
in front of their mouths by officials
when they had audience   certain leaves
fall long crisp like red halved sausages
roasted to a turn this autumn for the sidewalks
of New York of the occupants of the taxis
of the imitation of wealth thru the exhaust
girdle pendants   back scratchers with ivory handles
cages for singing and fighting crickets

* Imitation: *Mus.* The repetition of a phrase or subject in another
voice-part or in a different key.

56

18

The mirror oval sabres   playing
at chips in the room
next door   the voices behind the wall
will be lit by high lights in the morning

in bed a wall between continuing voices
chips stacking   instead of bales
the water sounds extending a harbor
one sleepless one sleeper on the fourth floor

19

Checkers, checkmate and checkerboard,
Confused are *checkerboard* and *chess*;
Shall whose writing be on paper
Whose move is on the checkerboard?

If red of a set have each a wreath
Each black checker should be wreathed:
Noble typing will make the writing
Her breath is his, to type "checkmate bequeathed."

20

Ears beringed with fuzz

owned a man's sculpturing head

autumn's regard

for weather like spring

holed shoes meeting pavement

If, when,

introduce these to

a fuzzed flower   Petal will

declare as of carving   "bluish soles'

walk, head, ears' hair: greeting"

21

Snows' night's winds on the window rattling
Would seem to leap out of the bed-spring

What prevents a feat like that occurring
Reason—but the more actual bedding

Springs of steel mercurial spirallings
Making a body's night a changeable singing

The winged boots of the frozen seek of it! sheltering
Safety from the window's pommelling

        To my wash-stand
in which I wash
        my left hand
and my right hand

        To my wash-stand
whose base is Greek
        whose shaft
is marble and is fluted

        To my wash-stand
whose wash-bowl
        is an oval
in a square

        To my wash-stand
whose square is marble
        and inscribes two
smaller ovals to left and right for soap

        Comes a song of
water from the right faucet and the left
        my left and my
right hand mixing hot and cold

        Comes a flow which
if I have called a song
        is a song
entirely in my head

        a song out of imagining
modillions descried above
        my head   a frieze
of stone completing what no longer

        is my wash-stand
since its marble has completed

        my getting up each morning
my washing before going to bed

        my look into a mirror
to glimpse half an oval
        as if its half
were half-oval in my head   and the

        climates of many
inscriptions human heads shapes'
        horses' elephants' (tusks) others'
scratched in marble tile

        so my wash-stand
in one particular breaking of the
        tile at which I have
looked and looked

        has opposed to my head
the inscription of a head
        whose coinage is the
coinage of the poor

        observant in waiting
in their getting up mornings
        and in their waiting
going to bed

        carefully attentive
to what they have
        and to what they do not
           have

when a flow of water
        doubled in narrow folds
occasions invertible counterpoints
        over a head   and

        an age in a wash-stand
and in their own heads

23

"The Immediate Aim"

1

Other than propaganda—

a police dog sniffs one;
a *German* police dog
not responsible for Naziism?
One is not sweet on him.

When one does not love animals,
one's concern is not respect.

Workers,
you could
take time off
this March morning

trot out
like this police dog

ambling critic
of spring

(the curse of verse on him!)

might make bare your eyes
to the white gull
astigmatically a launch

since it sits, distant
in the middle of the river:

your value which enslaves you
in advance

has made your eye-pupils limited—

inanity
to prate
the injustice of it.

2

Can dogs
argue
injustices

Dogs in a vise,
and a wood saw
can saw an anatomy
of dog

Such as you never saw.

If it yowls
shut the eyelid on a bad dream,
Let not the snarls take,
With its virus in you
You are immune.

What hounds
you means to.
Not all woodsawyers
grow animal.

3

Shanty
on the river
with
one window

The unemployed
having
a home
has no home

and no nag
protected
by
the United States' flag—

each animal
his own gravedigger
almost
sings

who will
walk out
against
the

social
and political
order of
things

24
This Fall, 1933

THE AMERICAN BANKNOTE FACTORY
    makes bills
The lights are on thru its basement,
    10 times 10 squared down the windows of its façade.

A boy with a rabbit in hand could no more
Caress it for his benumbed fingers, than if
    The drafts from the outside blew in noon and midnight,

Stormed green bills on the fall's leaves, the bills
Could caress them, make New York pavement less
    Bereavement, heyday out of moneyed inflation.

25

No One Inn

P.S.   i.e.   almost dreamt
the face against the door
a pastel's   a boy's

who owns it   being in a war
plays the market early
hires a chef   would look at his chef's hat

flour not at the exchange of
the exchanges   the margin drops
gets the chef walking   and preparing

it a cork   please,
be it, whose thought is it
floated   and by a house-boat

if there   wound 's sleep, to be sure
"then bacteria in mercurochrome?"—yes
if you want peroxide I will give you—thrive

the windings   an inn
the windings   a face in an inn
the windings   no one is in in No One Inn

26

A Junction

To such of one body as one mind

Whose ear shouts to ear separation,

Across the mean levels of oceans,

      Cities,—

To them a sight thru windows

      Which will not last,

The heart, and an arm—if it should conduct

      Remembering.

27

Song—¾ time
(pleasantly drunk)

Right out
      of
        Das Kapital

vol. I
    chap. 3
        2.
         A

"who has
      a
       taste

"for something
        that will
          warm
            up"

snow
    for
        my friend's birthday

I've
   been climbing
             every
                little

highway
       snow without—
              He

dances
     it
     —without—
           any money

(his
   friend's
       nose

is
 at
   the
     window

for the
     snow
        sparrows

in the
     junk
       heap
         of snow)

with
   a
   girl

over
    every
        little
           highway

of
  Spain
      for—

"there
      develops
             a
               multiplicity

"of
  social
      relations

"that are
      spontaneous in
             their
               growth

"and are
      quite
          outside

"the
    control of
          the
            actors"

"When
      one commodity
             replaces another

"the
  money
      commodity
         always

"remains
        in
            the hands

"of
    some
        third
            person"

"Circulation
                sweats money
                        unceasingly

"at every pore."
                "because the
                        weaver has sold
                                linen;

"the distiller
            is only able to
                    sell the strong

"waters
        because the
                bible agent has already

"sold the waters
                of
                    —
                        life;

"and
    so
        on."

"Specifically, a writer of music." The composite of notes proceeded with assumed qualities in a definite proportion. But, as dreamed, they controlled the nature of plants, bodies, etc., and the elements of the notes became not easy to separate. And, on the large muscle of the back, which passes from the spine to the head, they were settling longitudinally, like the wings of certain insects, where in the large opening of the roof in the ancient house stood the air.

He stood and turned the palm of the hand downward and backward, and like the notes the movement was extended in time. This act became a test of his powers. His body was published abroad, and like the Titan, long after him, whose liver renewed itself at night, it renewed itself on a long promenade in the mornings of days, the notes always the principal effort of his performance. He saw no one—only flowers, branches and buds developing from unusual places.

Till where the stamens combined by their filaments to form two bundles, he saw her, the power of authority upon her head. But her crown was a crown of his notes, so that she was immediately separate from him, as the notes were separate from her in what seemed to him their conversation in which she did yet did not take part. She disappeared into the brush.

And he heard himself saying, "For, I am at least half blind, my windows are all as full of glasses of waters as any mountebanks stall" on a field crowded with dancing donkeys. Half-crazed, he was running into them, seeking always the daughter of the governor of Seville. Stamping over him, the hoofs of the donkeys delivered, themselves delivered, the body of Don Giovanni to the devil. And as the field was impaired upon the point of their receding vision, the ever falling stomping of their hoofs, now following the range of his notes, were imparting to him clearly: "Sir, not only a mathematique point flowers into every line which is derived from a Center, but our soul which is but one, hath swallowed up a negative."

And now a dancing-master named Fox, but very gentle,—the music becoming a shallow, rounded depression. Gentle, and an irritant almost hard to be conscious of. So that the simplest fact of his life, "specifically, a writer of music," was beginning to mean very little. And for years it was four o'clock,—not time which would have broken the hour and placed a statue of David in history, but an ornamental herb of that name,—with flowers that grow in Peru of a great variety of color. So that for years it was four o'clock and the same as bloom from 4 P.M. till the next morning. And since there was a memory of the hoofs of donkeys who had left him, there could now be the sum of three and one, and of twice two. The groups came in four units: a team of four horses, a playing card with four spots, quadrupled measures, a bedstead with four posts, a four-wheeler allowing passage in any-one of four directions. Golf for a foursome. In rows of townships, six miles in width, between two meridian lines, isolated groups composed of sympathetic individuals who had given free play to all the feelings and passions had reached the doldrums of Fourier-ism, but without success. In their hearths the phosphorescence of foxwood, and he was a bystander. They were foxtrotting, two couples and four friends, two friends and four couples, between a pace and a walk, between a pace and a walk. He could see the upper-leather of their shoes along the edges next the soles. They moved very gently and sadly.

He was in his own time, his fears too much aroused and pro-longed, teased by repeated disappointments in the attainment of his object. If his notes could not extricate themselves from this complicated mass, they would be to his tactility like meeting at a point without further coincidence or intersection. If they did extricate themselves, they would, moving towards a definite shape, become capable of being apprehended, themselves their own ex-istence in the plain of surrounding existence, tactility of materials become tangible. Lao-tse was working a Chinese puzzle consisting of a square cardboard cut by straight incisions into five triangles, a square and a lozenge—combining them into a variety of figures. It was a relief from ethics, an approach to the blue huckleberry. The tap-dancer was not a Chinaman. He was in a trench plunged to his neck in water, the fruit hanging above him. On a level with it a caterpillar tractor was pecking away at an acre of earth. Foolish, but there was the tap-dancer singing:

> Taps nailed upon the heel of shoe
> Make the water tantivy, tantivy, tantivy

Then he danced out very clearly and swiftly:

> My instep in the stirrup's
> tapadera

The tap-dancer was tapering towards the head, in a column of water growing conical, around, and containing, him. He heard a woman using a medicine composed of an ingredient of tansy say: One of the principal applications of tannic acid is in the prepara-tion of writing-ink. He turned the tap-dance into a tango passing out in a diagonal shuffle.

Whirl, dip, and a swing! The duenna is a dragon! What is it, inflexible Draco, that is fabulous, has wings unlike a serpent, and is a monster! Come on! Come on! drag your brains! The Northern constellation? Guess again! A short, large-bored firearm of the 17th century or the soldier who carried it? That was before your time, what do you know about it? The small arboreal Asiatic lizard (genus *Draco*!) leaps aided by a parachute formed by lateral expansions of the skin supported by elongated and extensible hind ribs. What shall we say of the little flying lizards, what of the metamorphosis of the dragonfly, its four large wings and enormous eyes? Shall we call them with fourfold-thought of gentleness the devil's darning needle. The dragon is a duenna! The dragon has an inner paddle-shaft like a marine engine! The dragon is an excavator that draws the soil upward and away from the working-base thus clearing it. Scripturally, *tannim*, the meaning of which is uncertain. There went up a smoke out of his nostrils, and fire out of his mouth devoured: coals were kindled by it.—Wounds stink.—Caused men to ride over our heads. As smoke is driven away, so drive them away. (To the chief Musician, Psalms 18, 38, 66, 68!)

29

N.Y.

"At heaven's gate" the larks: have
Read to date the nth reversion, "re" Marx

Of the mind's image   a hangar
A red crane—on the nearby wharves

In the spring-blue day—not working
But not out of languor

January the 29 , the 29th birthday
Falling on a Sunday

As planned there should be to-day
29 songs written over two years

And with, but without expected, pay

I have written down twenty-three
Leaving 5 and another page blank

To record a January without snow
For the delectation of the file and rank.

"Further than"—

Further than the wash-stand
three mountains in one bathroom
The mountains on the floor, sea-bed
rock, colored design; Five figures, chance
smudges, perhaps tar, in the mountains; Six
and Five figures in the waters under
and above them. Each figure
is an ordinate of which the axis

is a peak, The Whole Peak, from summit
thru base to inverted altitude, depth beneath
sea level. Only drying from the shower is
exploration possible, the chances
of world monopoly have been so carefully
seized that only on the other side of
one's bathroom nothing is foreign. Unless
charting the antarctic has something to do
with figures the heads of which are
just smudges away from the axis of abscissas
or one is merely exploring from a shower
expectant that today or tomorrow must
bring the new economic anatomization.

"Mantis"

Mantis! praying mantis! since your wings' leaves
And your terrified eyes, pins, bright, black and poor
Beg—"Look, take it up" (thoughts' torsion)! "save it!"
I who can't bear to look, cannot touch,—You—
You can—but no one sees you steadying lost
In the cars' drafts on the lit subway stone.

Praying mantis, what wind-up brought you, stone
On which you sometimes prop, prey among leaves
(Is it love's food your raised stomach prays?), lost
Here, stone holds only seats on which the poor
Ride, who rising from the news may trample you—
The shops' crowds a jam with no flies in it.

Even the newsboy who now sees knows it
No use, papers make money, makes stone, stone,
Banks, "it is harmless," he says moving on—You?
Where will he put *you*? There are no safe leaves
To put you back in here, here's news! too poor
Like all the separate poor to save the lost.

Don't light on my chest, mantis! do—you're lost,
Let the poor laugh at my fright, then see it:
My shame and theirs, you whom old Europe's poor

Call spectre, strawberry, by turns; a stone—
You point—they say—you lead lost children—leaves
Close in the paths men leave, saved, safe with you.

Killed by thorns (once men), who now will save you
Mantis? what male love bring a fly, be lost
Within your mouth, prophetess, harmless to leaves
And hands, faked flower,—the myth is: dead, bones, it
Was assembled, apes wing in wind: On stone,
Mantis, you will die, touch, beg, of the poor.

Android, loving beggar, dive to the poor
As your love would even without head to you,
Graze like machined wheels, green, from off this stone
And preying on each terrified chest, lost
Say, I am old as the globe, the moon, it
Is my old shoe, yours, be free as the leaves.

Fly, mantis, on the poor, arise like leaves
The armies of the poor, strength: stone on stone
And build the new world in your eyes, Save it!

"Mantis," An Interpretation

or Nomina sunt consequentia rerum,
names are sequent to the things named

Mantis! praying mantis! since your wings' leaves
> Incipit Vita Nova
> le parole . . .
> almeno la loro sentenzia
the words . . .
at least their substance

at first were
"The mantis opened its body
It had been lost in the subway
It steadied against the drafts
It looked up—
Begging eyes—

74

It flew at my chest"

       —The ungainliness
       of the creature needs stating.

No one would be struck merely
By its ungainliness,
Having seen the thing happen.

Having seen the thing happen,
There would be no intention 'to write it up,'

But *all* that was happening,
The mantis itself only an incident, *compelling any writing*
The transitions were perforce omitted.

Thoughts'—two or three or five or
Six thoughts' reflection (pulse's witness) of what was happening
All immediate, not moved by any transition.

Feeling this, what should be the form
Which the ungainliness already suggested
Should take?

       —Description—lightly—ungainliness
       With a grace unrelated to its surroundings.

Grace there is perhaps
In the visual sense, not in the movement of
"eyes, pins, bright, black and poor."

Or considering more than the isolation
Of one wrenched line,

Consider:
"(thoughts' torsion)"
la battaglia delli diversi pensieri . . .
the battle of diverse thoughts—
The actual twisting
Of many and diverse thoughts

75

What form should *that* take?
>   —The first words that came into mind
>   "The mantis opened its body—"
>   Which might deserve the trope:
>   the feeling of the original which is a permanence

>   ?

Or the feeling accompanying the first poor 27 words' inception
(the original which is a permanence
?),
That this thoughts' torsion
Is really a sestina
Carrying subconsciously
Many intellectual and sensual properties of the
>   forgetting and remembering Head
One human's intuitive Head

>   **Dante's rubric**
>   **Incipit**
>   **Surrealiste**
>   **Re-collection**

A twisted shoe by a pen, an insect, lost,
"To the short day and the great sweep of shadow."

The sestina, then, the repeated end words
Of the lines' winding around themselves,
Since continuous in the Head, whatever has been read,
>   whatever is heard,
>   whatever is seen
Perhaps goes back cropping up again with
Inevitable recurrence again in the blood
Where the spaces of verse are not visual
But a movement,
With vision in the lines merely a movement.

What is most significant
Perhaps is that C—and S—and X—of the 19th century
Used the "form"—not the form but a Victorian
Stuffing like upholstery

For parlor polish,
And our time takes count against them
For their blindness and their (unintended?) cruel smugness.

Again: as an experiment, the sestina would be wicker-work—
As a force, one would lie to one's feelings not to use it

One feels in fact inevitably
About the coincidence of the mantis lost in the subway,
About the growing oppression of the poor—
Which is the situation most pertinent to us—,
With the fact of the sestina:
Which together fatally now crop up again
To twist themselves anew
To record not a sestina, post Dante,
Nor even a mantis.

Is the poem then, a sestina
Or not a sestina?

The word sestina has been
Taken out of the original title. It is no use (killing oneself?)

      —Our world will not stand it,
      the implications of a too regular form.

Hard to convince even one likely to show interest in the matter
That this regularity to which 'write it up' means not a damn

(Millet in a Dali canvas, Circe in E's Cantos)
Whatever seeming modelling after the event,
649 years, say, after Dante's first canzone,
If it came back immediately as the only
Form that will include the most pertinent subject of our day—
The poor—
Cannot mean merely implied comparison, unreality
Usually interpreted as falsity.

Too much time cannot be saved
Saying:
The mantis might have heaped up upon itself a
Grave of verse,

But the facts are not a symbol.

There is the difference between that
And a fact (the mantis in the subway)
And all the other facts the mantis sets going about it.

No human being wishes to become
An insect for the sake of a symbol.

But the mantis *can start*
History etc.
The mantis situation remains its situation,
Enough worth if the emotions can equate it,

"I think" of the mantis
"I think" of other things—
The quotes set repulsion
Into movement.

Repulsion—
Since one, present, won't touch the mantis,
Will even touch the poor—

but carefully.

The mantis, then,
Is a small incident of one's physical vision
Which is the poor's helplessness
The poor's separateness
Bringing self-disgust.

The mantis is less ungainly than that.

There should be to-day no use for a description of it
Only for a "movement" emphasizing its use, since it's been around,

An accident in the twisting
Of many and diverse "thoughts"
i.e. nerves, glandular facilities, electrical cranial charges
For example—
line 1—entomology
line 9—biology

lines 10 and 11—the even rhythm of riding under-
              ground, and the sudden jolt are also
              of these nerves, glandular facilities,
              brain's charges
line 12—pun, fact, banality
lines 13 to 18—the economics of the very poor—the
              newsboy—unable to think beyond
              "subsistence still permits competi-
              tion," banking, *The Wisconsin Elkhorn
              Independent*—"Rags make paper,
              paper makes money, money makes
              banks, banks make loans, loans make
              poverty, poverty makes rags."
lines 22 to 24—Provence myth
lines 25 to 29—Melanesian self-extinction myth
line 33—airships
lines 35 and 36—creation myth (Melanesia), residue of
              it in our emotions no matter if fetched
              from the moon, as against l. 25 to 29.
and naturally the coda which is the
only thing that can sum up the
jumble of order in the lines weaving
"thoughts," pulsations, running commentary, one upon the other,
itself a jumble of order
as far as poetic
sequence is concerned:

              the mantis
              the poor's strength
              the new world.

39—"in your eyes"
              the original shock still persisting—

So that the invoked collective
Does not subdue the senses' awareness,
The longing for touch to an idea, or
To a use function of the material:
The original emotion remaining,
      like the collective,
Unprompted, real, as propaganda.

The voice exhorting, trusting what one hears
Will exhort others, is the imposed sensuality of an age

When both propaganda and sensuality are necessary against—
"—we have been left with nothing
just a few little unimportant ships
and barges" (British Admiralty even in 1920)

or jelly for the Pope

la mia nemica, madonna la pieta
my enemy, my lady pity,

36—"like leaves"
The Head remembering these words exactly in the way it
                                                    remembers
la calcina pietra
the calcined stone.

But it remembers even more constantly
the poor
than
com' huom pietra sott' erba
as one should hide a stone in grass.

Nor is the coincidence
Of the last four lines
Symbolism,
But the simultaneous,
The diaphanous, historical
In one head.

                                    November 4, 1934
                                    New York

The six blank pages intended by Song 29, written January 29th, 1933, were filled during 1933 and the early months of 1934 with songs 11, 23, 24, 26, 27, 28. Added to the original collection their number is not included in, or for, the title of the book, namely *55 Poems*. They are dedicated rather by their subjects.

Anew

1

che di lor suona su nella tua vita

> I walked out, before
> "Break of day"
> And saw
> Four cabins in the hay.
>
> Blue sealed glasses
> Of preserves—four—
> In the window-sash
> In the yard on the bay.
>
> Further:
> The waters
> At the ramp
> Running away.

2

One lutenist played *look;* your thought was *drink:*
Then why like him pledge her to see?
Ben, all clocks stop in a house-party's eyes.
Music avoids impossibility.

If lonely she go with me from this room
We will look where lute notes dispose,
Whether from some rebellious dead, or still
One more earth where the marsh-marigold grows.

3

The green plant grows
Says your old man
But the white pot it is in
    Does not grow
The thorns are the roses'.

My old man's beard
Is older than your old man's,
And whatever song, the winds,
    And the snow,
Older than their prose is.

Went a lande a
Ship of Lusseboene but that lande
. . . All thinges is comune*
    As we know
As their suns' our sons' closes.

* Amerigo Vespucci

4

So sounds grass, and if it is sun or no sun
Sun on bur, or a noise in the ear's burr
A long sleep, and a full stillness.
It is Light. Circles

            star.

           Bur,
           Sum,

If they ask, it is you
Never with wilfulness,

A high fire fills a trench.
Sum, Egypt was a Sum, knows you as
Trench mortar and pyramids.

Sum, you are constructed, as of the tides, of your voice,
Water has this constancy, illness nothing,
By cheek bones
As of two as of many in the hills of Teruel

The guns of the loyal arms
Leaving the hands hanging from branches in snow,
River bottoms
And their shores where river bottoms were.

5

Ah spring, when with a thaw of blue
Sun in the street will she be as to-day?
Seaplane up to sky over sky
Avenues without empire an earth of May.

6

Anew, sun, to fire summer
leaves move toward the air
from the stems of the branches

        fire summer   fire summer

but for the people cheated
from the birds heard singing
thru four months on shore
toward the people in the waves

the green leaves that fill up the day
and those eaten away
—point-lace worked over a stem—
blow up on the trees of the cliff

on the top
the mill with the clock-tower
fires summer
        over a midsummer shore.

7

When the crickets
sound like fifty water-taps
forsaken at once

the inclemency
of the inhuman noises
is the earth's

with its roadways
over cabins in the forests

the sheets smell
of sweet milk

all the waters
of the world

we are going
to sleep to sleep

8

Has the sum
Twenty-five
Reduced the years
Of the live songs
To one-quarter
Of a century
Become cold mortar
Of a pyramid?
   Forget the number
Think of an entablature of snow
Engraved there 2 a bird-prow
Taking 5 in tow,
Then Ra look down

The figure shining thru the measure
Each song the midday
A sum of each year's leisure.

9

For you I have emptied the meaning
Leaving the song
Or would a god—a god of midday
Have been brought in by the neck
For foes to peck at

God the man is so overweening
He would prolong
A folly of thought see 2 as a bird
And what not that we rid day of
So that we may think in our time

Two birds tip on the guy wire
The green rained on
Is coppered by sunset, a treeling's
So black (together we hush a response) between
Its trunk and silk mesh of kirtle showed evening.

10

What are these songs
straining at sense—
you the consequence?

11

In the midst of things
One scotch and soda, and
Happy birthday! have you
Been walking in DICKEYVILLE
EIGHTEENTH CENTURY
DEVELOPMENT?
They turned
The walls of an old mill
There into a house.

VOICE OF THE HOUSE-DOOR
(Speaking after Catullus):
Sees all—
Time brings the guy with red eyebrows
In love with the Mrs. of this house
Who had her husband
After she had had his father.

(Pitying itself considerably)
Dazh the nizhest poem
I ever wrote exshepting
All the other nizher poems.

12

It's hard to see but think of a sea
Condensed into a speck.
And there are waves—
Frequencies of light,
Others that may be heard.
The one is one sea, the other a second.
There are electric stresses across condensers
That wear them down till they can stand no strain,
Are of no force and as unreclaimed
       as the bottom of the sea

Unless the space the stresses cross be air,
        that can be patched.
Large and small condensers,
Passing in the one instance frequencies
        that can be turned to sound,
In the other, alternations that escape,
So many waves of a speck of sea or what,
Or a graph the curve of a wave beyond all sound,
An open circuit where no action—
Like that of the retina made human by light—
Is recorded otherwise
Than having taken a desired path a little way
And tho infinitely a mote to be uncontained for
        ever.
This science is then like gathering flowers of the
        weed
One who works with me calls birdseed
That are tiny and many on one stem
They shed to the touch tho on a par
        with the large flower
That picked will find a vase.
I see many things at one time
        the harder the concepts get,
Or nothing
Which is a forever become me over forty years.
I am like another, and another, who has
        finished learning
And has just begun to learn.
If I turn pages back
A child may as well be staring with me
Wondering at the meaning
I turn to last
Perhaps.

13

A last cigarette
a companion

dark, spring's
green smells

and the work
is in mind

a love's
unclouding it

the spontaneous
idea

is not yet
called up

a green light
of the subway
entrance

to let spring ask
is the world

at the World's Fair
any more
than an action sings.

Science, too, posted
after all smells

carefully fostering
cadres

not grudging
time

patiently
"bothering."

"One oak fool box";—the pun
Retrieved from past days
Will soon be quicker than the thronged
Waiting room of the terminal in the dimout
In time of war,
When three trains leave within
          a minute of each other
For the same place:—
Here simmer the stray words of friends,
Guise of an agitation of electrical storms,
The accelerated impulse and emotion
               of events
Under the immense vault with
          extinguished bulbs,
In the granite columns
That derive unwieldy acanthus:—
The pun born of an oak file,
Of an aimless card index where there
                 was peace:—
Dooley said:—and not so damned mute—
When the story of a great battle is written,
They'll print the killed,
The wounded, the missing,
And the seriously disturbed:—
As if some ancient head
Or its plaster cast,
Colorless water,
Said:—
If number, measure and weighing
Be taken away from any art,
That which remains will not be much:—
At least nothing like an
Appreciation of dawn
After the sixth day of work in one week:—
Or of snow melting from trees
If it falls with a sound of leaves.

No it was no dream of coming death,
Those you love will live long.
If light hurried my dream, I saw none:
Stepped from my bed and to the sill,
From a window looked down
On the river I knew set forth
To rise toward me—full after rain.
People watched, crowded the banks, thought
As with old words to a river:
(Whose waters seemed unwillingly
to glide like friends who linger while
they sever.) Soon, as expected!
A coffin launched like a ship's hull
Sped as from a curtain afire
Draped to the keystone of an arch
And—as at a burial at sea—
Sank. The displaced water rose,
Made the heart sound the coffin's grave,
Woke under the stream and in me
A set of furtive bells, muted
And jangling by rote "What does this say?
What loss will make the world different?
Are they gathered to further war?
What sorrow do you fear?
Ask, will you, is it here
Distrust is cast off, all
Cowardice dies. Eyes, looking out,
Without the good of intellect,
Rouse as you are used to:
It is the bad fallen away,
And the sorrow in the good.
 You saw now for your book, *Anew.*"

I walk in the old street
to hear the beloved songs
afresh
this spring night.

Like the leaves—my loves wake—
not to be the same
or look tireless to the stars
and a ripped doorbell.

Guillaume de Machault (1300–1377)
Ballade: Plourès, dames

Cry for me, ladies, your servant
        Who said all he
May, I leave heart and intent,

Heart, my desire and thought, as your servant,
        To honor you
Whom God keep and augment.

        Dress yourselves in black for me,
        My heart fails my pale look (you see)
Death is all I see of this adventure
        If God and you
Do not take me for sure.

The bird that cries like a baby
Is the crow
Or a softer voice.
The turning spray of cypress
The seeming evergreen
With red falls of Virginia creeper
Nears the red of forsythia
That with the season lost its yellow.
Crickets keep filing away.
Forsythia named *Golden-rain* of parks
Appears wild in the country.
How like the west is the east
The sun setting sooner:
A tulip-tree by itself makes the autumnal east golden.
Before the clock was turned back an hour
This morning and it stopped saving daylight
A rescript was heard—
Caw—
Of the oldest Throne's baby,
"To enhance justice on earth
    and to make the world one household . . . "

Swimming in the creek
Water is colder and older.

And so till we have died
And grass with grass
Lie faceless as the grass

Grow sheathed with the grass
Between our spines a hollow
The stillest sense will pass
Or weighted cloud will follow.

The lines of this new song are nothing
But a tune making the nothing full
Stonelike become more hard than silent
The tune's image holding in the line.

Can a mote of sunlight defeat its purpose
When thought shows it to be deep or dark?

See sun, and think shadow.

Catullus viii

Miserable Catullus, stop being foolish
And admit it's over,
The sun shone on you those days
When your girl had you
When you gave it to her
   like nobody else ever will.
Everywhere together then, always at it
And you liked it and she can't say
     she didn't
Yes, those days glowed.
Now she doesn't want it: why
    should you, washed out
Want to. Don't trail her,
Don't eat yourself up alive,
Show some spunk, stand up
     and take it.

So long, girl. Catullus
                        can take it.
He won't bother you, he won't
                        be bothered:
But you'll be, nights.
What do you want to live for?
Whom will you see?
Who'll say you're pretty?
Who'll give it to you now?
Whose name will you have?
Kiss what guy? bite whose
                        lips?
Come on Catullus, you can
                        take it.

23

Gulls over a rotting hull,
Past a bridge their wings annul,
Are such fact the time must see:
Where no bridge spans war's decree,
Birds do, sea, ruin, burial.

24

The men in the kitchens
Their women in the foundries
The children in the wars
The old men at the boundaries.

for
Zadkine

It is a hard thing to say that when I first saw
La Prisonnière I wanted to run
And that I did, only that some birds then sang
In your courtyard, pursuing me
Over stone where you work in stone,
To come upon the prisoner in a field again.
Grass overgrowing ruins of the war
Over which she sprang, her head for other hours,
        above a wrecked column—
Like none that had ever been—
Nailed together maybe from broken curbs of wells,
        wood once now stone:
There, she was the Furies sometime called kind
Where the haunted stop on a ray of sun
Tho the bird still dreamed of pursues—
Any bird, that is, over a gravestone
Or a grave lacking one.
In the art of stone it is hard to set one's own
        seal upon the idea of stone,
And in a world from which most
        ideas have gone
To take the wreck of its idea
And make it stone
Raised up as a column
In which the prisoner is meant to be,
Over seas and fields and years,
Beside Daphne in the tree
And like a tree
But of stone to be seen in the sun,
Is harder.
There are almost no friends
But a few birds to tell what you have done.

26
1892–1941

To be moved comes of want, tho want be complete
as understanding. Cast, the statue rests, stopped:
a bronze—not "Grief"—the drapery should take in
body and head. The working eyes discarded.

Characterless lips, straight nose, sight, form no clue
(are none too great sculpture) to portrait or you.
At the seat of government, but a cab's jaunt
from the evergreens raised about the statue,

people count, climb the steps of the Capitol.
Shrubs, close to hands, that age at the visitor's
curved bench derive no clue from its smooth stone or
its simplicity or animal foot ends.

Nor shows the headstone back of the figure's seat
more than a blank emblem of two wreaths entwined,
bare in Eighteen Ninety Two, of our country.
Dark forearm not draped, hand modeled to the chin:

a lady of Nineteen Forty One met by
chance, asked where you could be found, took us three here,
left quickly, said, "The two of them lie there"

(I am one alive while two see here with me)

under the circle of purposeful gravel
feet must skirt or cross to come near the figure
over the gravel as on no other plot, in
"the cemetery known as Rock Creek": the name

gravel, those under. "One's instinct abhors time."

A madrigal for 3 voices

Hail the tree's meadow
Where the watch
Fees no property

    Where bread crumbs strike
      Red raked leaves
    Pigeons redden shadow
      Under red feet

          When pigeons greet
Workers meeting—
In the valley
      of the city—
Not a chimney's
      made of putty
And the lampposts
      are high
        high
           and white—or
         red, like
no property of
      night.

28

The rains, the rains
Toward spring pour thru
The winter night
And freeze to hail.

Seasoned armies
Tested in defeat
Retreating now
In that order

They cannot yield,
No more than weather
Of their hemisphere:
The rain that turns

To hail before
The thunderstorms,
The rains, the rains
Of spring call out.

29

Glad they were there
Falling away
Flying not to
Lose sight of it
Not going far
In angles out
Of ovals of
Dances filled up
The field the green
With light above
With the one hand
In the other.

30

A marriage song
for
Florence and Harry

Be happy you two
    Whose one aim
Makes the bride take
    The bridegroom's name.

As the birds on the hedge.
    Nor edge
Away in time
To ask how two
    May be
    Happy.

31

My nephew
And my new
Niece

Joy
On their wedding

From his mother
My sister
He never saw
And my mother
Her mother
Hers

    not to see

From my father
And his father

To the bride
Whatever she be

From the unconcerned
Dancers
Today

From the streets
From the walls
Of their house
Tomorrow

From where
He works

From the hills
From the sea

What if a thousand
Has been thrown
Away

Leaves of the fall
Gold

Blow away

Joy
On their wedding

Love tomorrow
Loved today

32

Even if love convey
His line, his tone,
We see him, alone,
Dissatisfied,
Tonight near yesterday.

See in his art
This tone the sun
And in this line his living eyes.
All was in place with him,
My valentine.

Even while on our green wall
His painting hangs
And makes new our will, oh
All artlessness cries:
"Sleep fast, I need the pillow!"

33

Drive, fast kisses,
no need to see
hands or eyelashes
a mouth at her ear
trees or leaves
night or the days.

34

The Letter of Poor Birds

The letter of poor birds
Is a wish or a song:
If we can be more, should we
On uninteresting land?
Today we saw hollows and low crests
The fallow, the arid, and the growing patch,
The yellow root of a red shrub
    make winter rosy
And cast such shadow on a white cottage.
The sparrows cram bread and drink. Do we
Drink more than water that flaws a drain?
You will believe they sang:
Jerry, Paul, Celia, Louis.

35

Or a valentine

What I did not say the other day to you for today
Is not unsaid because lost today with such thoughts
                in my head
That make one who looks up at the time say it has
                gone ahead.

36

        Strange
To reach that age,
              remember
    a tide
And full
    for a time
           be young.

37

The world autumn
Spiked seeds on undried branches
The tufted clouds
Where you look
So many falls for you
In the river
And where earth gives
Under each shoe

Past slate rock
You will see what soft blue is
With the sea
Such eyes as you have

38

Belly Locks Shnooks Oakie
When he awoke, he
Scared all the spooks. He
Was some oak, he
        Was.

39

One friend,
Red sealing wax, can say of us,
Their house—a woman and a man
Ate food and talked
Prolonged it but

To write, to sing:

White wax, dear face, Love,
Carry my child,—
Taper,—
Point us like any
Two plants.

40

Celia's birthday poem

No ache, love, 's the way to start the New Year,—
chant, then, "New Year" like "No ache" in your ear,
all the while I praise wind and love your face
above snow that melts over trees' space:
carol "No ache" like "New Year" between trees
that removed still share a few centuries.

41

After Charles Sedley

Not, Celia, that I look for rest
    In what I do or am;
In its own time this song addressed
    To you is not for them:

The hurrying world, our hastes have
    No part in you like me;
Faces stop showing what they crave
    In my attempt to see.

"All that in woman is adored"
    Grows my phrase, and your mind
Sings some hundreds of years to afford
    My cadence in kind.

And if your ears hear me I store
    It in our book *Anew*
Where we last who make Sedley—more
    Than he was perhaps—true.

You three:—my wife,
    And the one, whom like Dante,
    I call the chief of my friends,

And the one who still writes to me—
    This morning we are in the mess of history,
    That low crime, and like the devil in the book of *Job*

Having come back from going to and fro in the earth
    I will give the world all my hushed sources
    In this poem, (maybe the world wanted them)

I will be so frank everyone
    Will be sure I am hiding—a maniac—
    And no one will speak to me.

In any case, if it happens,
    I will not regret it one day
    That I am plain to the simplest.

But you three: my friend, my wife, and you,
    On whom my face and words weigh
    For whom pavement becomes too vague

To walk on because of me
    For whom the cracks in our plastered walls
    Cry out for me "I die! die!"

So that you want to shut your ears,
    Who begin to judge that something like my stars
    Weep on us the falls of black luck,

Who must be like myself and not pity me
    (I am, after all, of the people whose wisdom
    May die with them)

Who on top of the years cannot stand the thought
  That my tears too can be wet—
  I will ape a dead poet for you

And tell you of the little spirits of sight
  And the eyes, the beginning of love,
  And of the mouth which is its goal,

And of the appetite, he called heart
  And the reason, 'I call soul'.
  These words are better than I

And if I do die before you, as I have always
    wished,—
  Why, that's nothing new, I have always wished
    it,—
  They may speak to you, the equal

Of your own great anxiety
  As when I should have slept
  This morning and you were awake:

"He walks into door-jambs
  Never sees
  Where he goes

"He must do so many things
  In the morning, shower, brush,
  Clean his glasses a half dozen times,

"Pare his toe nails and cut his toes
  Remove the dirt from his finger nails
  After washing (for a clean person!)

"Shave with a dull blade, bolt breakfast,
  That after all night
  Reaching for his pocket flashlight,

"The kind they use in this war,
  To light up the face of his wrist watch
  'two-thirty'—after going

"To bed at two—
    'Two-fifteen'!
    'Three-fifteen, four o'clock,

" 'It is almost time to get up
    I haven't slept, I don't
    Think I will'—out loud!"

"Please"—"Okay! poet
    Did you ever get up
    Without aching

Without looking grouchy?
    You're not like your old father,
    Everyone looking at you would rather suffer instead of you."

I was thinking, shaving at the mirror,
    Will she write the music I cannot,
    Will he paint, probe, what I cannot

Will the other say the words that escape me?
    Will I, who must, write of my world's battle
    In which I have asked, and which I am not allowed,

To fight? Let your words be my testament.
    For I cannot believe we will not grow from them,
    When not needing even to conceive an aversion for anything

Despite the sage I will be dead
    And my thought in you for yet a while
    Wrapped in your words with a question—

Like that of Job's scourge—
    Do you know you are warmed in the earth
    By the south wind?

A beam of light, then, that you may still question.
    You three not divided, nor from me,
    In silence.

43

To my baby Paul

(After Guido)

Since we can't go back to Tuscany, Dinty,
We'll drink to you and Celia and to Jerry
And place her there who has never seen a
                         vineyard—
Drinking Chianti with us for the days
                    when you will be growing.

1

"che di lor suona su nella tua vita"
Continuing with Dante (limbo, THE INFERNO, IV, 77)

The comma in line 1 of this poem is meant as a pause in the expectancy of the dream. Perhaps the capital B of "Break," after the opening quotes of line 2, gives the feeling of some unexpected person taking part in one's expected activity: I was aware in the dream that I was writing a poem and also aware of verses by others.

The word "bay" is what I could reconstruct later from the feeling of the action in the dream, as I moved from place to place, and should convey something of all the meanings of the word "bay": red-brown, the laurel, the laurel wreath, a bay horse, a deep bark or cry, a window-bay, a large space in a barn for storage as of hay or fodder, the state of being kept at a standstill, but more specifically two meanings that seemed to include all the others, they are, an arm of the sea and a recess of low land between hills.

The "glasses of preserves" were sealed with white wax.

The waters teemed like flood waters, but perhaps this is an afterthought. They were certainly *falls*, tons of them off the side, on a curve, and nearly on the level of the ramp, and the ramp seemed to be running away at the curve.

When I awoke the exact words of the poem I dreamt were lost, but those I wrote down still seemed to follow on the events of the dream. Later, that morning, Dante's "which sounds of them, up in that life of thine" seemed an appropriate explanation.

29

"Glad they were there"

> . . . e quelle anime liete
> si fero spere sopra fissi poli,
> fiammando forte a guisa di comete
>
> cosi quelle carole differente-
> mente danzando, della sua ricchezza
> mi si facean stimar, veloci e lente.

PARADISO, XXIV, 10–12, 16–18.

. . . it is a contradiction to say that a body is continually falling towards another and is at the same time continually flying away from it. The ellipse is a trajectory which, while allowing this contradiction to subsist, at the same time solves it.

. . . the bodily substance of the gold counts only as the embodiment of value . . . In its reality, therefore, it is exchange-value. Its use-value manifests itself solely in the ideal form, in the series of expressions of relative value, in which it enters into relation with the contraposing commodities as the complex of its real use forms. These antagonistic forms of commodities are the real forms in which the process of their exchange has its movement and its being.

DAS KAPITAL, Metamorphosis of Commodities

. . . general theory of electromagnetic field, and in which we constantly have in view the state of matter or the medium by which the field is occupied. While speaking of this state, I must immediately call your attention to the curious fact that, although we never lose sight of it, we need by no means go far in attempting to form an image of it and, in fact, we cannot say much about it.

. . . The second assumption relates to a magnetic field. Without thinking of those hidden rotations of which I have just spoken, we can define this by the so called *magnetic force*, i.e. the force acting on a pole of unit strength.

. . . It is not the motion of a single electron, nor the field produced by it, that can make itself felt in our experiments, in which we are always concerned with immense numbers of particles; only the resultant effects produced by them are perceptible to our senses.

Henrik Anton Lorentz
THEORY OF ELECTRONS, pp. 1, 2, 133

. . . luce e sta verde
Guido Cavalcanti, MADRIGALE

Some Time

Some time has gone
Since these were written:
The cause runs off—
A child's mitten.

But hear play the
Fingers of his hand
Celia perpends—
To understand.

SEQUENCE 1944–6

1

I look at the pines on the hillside,
Alive,
And they not I who work
More or less absorbed
Have died.

2

But lose patience,
I lose patience.
Tied to song
Cannot speak.

We cross upon
One acre of music—
Asking
(So close who are cross)
Of acres and music:
Patience and time.

I am crazy about you

I feel
    sick.

Heart too human
To prefer the humane
That will not stop you
From beating again
And again

Wild

Thoughtful love
Crying, crying
Unreasoning child—

Having outlived self-offense
And that of my friends
I became brother to loneliness
And love the fact more than the wo‐ '

All that is human is
Alien and not alien.
All carefully chosen words
Are here—fairly shadows.

You have music to accord.
A child
At a remove from love
Holds leaves in my hand.

Where the world is headed
We do not say
As stars
Sun and surf

Flash in the sky. Were it said
Among twigs
"And then the world went
And then—"

Only our thoughts
Might seek it
In further woods.

5

(Flushing Meadows)

The flags in the water
Like grain that will not grow—
Out of the way
Out of the flow—

Silt and the sand
Where there is no harbor
Grow for the eye
That slows the hand.

A SONG FOR THE YEAR'S END

1

Daughter of music
and her sweet son
so that none rule
the dew to his own hurt
with the year's last sigh
awake
the starry sky and bird.

2

I shall go back to my mother's grave after this war
Because there are those who'll still speak of loyalty
In the outskirts of Baltimore
Or wherever Jews are not the right sort of people,
And say to her one of the dead I speak to—
There are less Jews left in the world,
While they were killed

I did not see you in a dream to tell you,
And that I now have a wife and son.

Then I shall go and write of my country,
Have a job all my life
Seldom write with grace again, be part of the world,
See every man in forced labor,
Dawn only where suburbs are *restricted*
To people who take trains every morning,
Never the gentleness that can be,
The hope of the common man, the eyes that love leaves
Any shade, thought or thing that makes all man uncommon,

But always the depraved bark
Fight or work,
Dawn the red poster, the advertiser's cock crow,
Sunset a lack of wonder, the lone winged foot of Mercury in
    tie with a tire,
The fashion model
Her train stopped in the railroad cut
Looking up to a billboard of herself
As she goes home to her small son asleep,

So early and so late in the fortunes that followed
    me from my mother's grave
A lovely air follows her
And the dead President who is worth it:
'Dear death, like peace, I end not speaking,
The chitchat has died
And the last smile is unwilled
I am dead, I can't talk
To blossoms or spring in the world.'

3

    "Because he was crying
I like him most of all," says my son
"Because he was crying,"—the red fox
With three porcupine quills in his paw—
Who brings tears to the eyes,
    button nose against shambles,

Valentines all day, all night, tomorrow
The simplest the keyboard can play,
'Pony gay, on your way,' love's hair
With two gray, Papa Bear's Song
    new to renew,
'Who's been sitting in my chair?'

QUE J'AY DIT DEVANT

1

Day that passes,
Day that stays,
Day that passes
Other days'

Crow's-foot, sieges,
Tears, bare way,
A god's egis,
Catspaw spray.

2

Marry or don't
(If you wish)

Weigh the way in May
Given to brighter green
                Than that seen
Thru white curtain.

Love, weigh the way
Green, coat this May's green.
                No wish seen
Is uncertain.

Kiss the child's hard cheek.
Draw from a light green
                Away, seen
Thru white curtain.

It is the way the cheek
Shocks a bright green
                    Makes it seen
Who is certain.

SO THAT EVEN A LOVER

1

Little wrists,
Is your content
My sight or hold,
Or your small air
That lights and trysts?

Red alder berry
Will singly break;
But you—how slight—do:
So that even
A lover exists.

2

Hello, little leaves,
Said not St. Francis
But my son in the spring,
Doing at two
(Neither really begged)
What it took the other—
He'd agree and laugh—
44 years to do.

LIGHT

1

An instruction booklet on a certain effect
    in which
Mass becomes o
Inertia approaches ∞

Light is critical
Time, immaterial
Distance, inside out.

2

A house where every
                    jigger
is in place
including
          a miniature outrigger
such peace
has no need
          to figure
out who pulled
          the trigger.

3

Because Tarzan triumphs
See Tarzan the He-man
Go to sleep with boy in jungle corral
And chimpanzee, the best man, delouse
By the bed, hear that movie goer's giggle!
Clean,
Tarzan gives up his bed
                    lush couch—
Thru with women: that girl
With her hair down in the world
Can take care of herself in his bed.

"Tarzan, boy's mother," he says slapping
The boy's rear, and
Reared by the jungle
He beats a man's breasts on his chest,
"He likes swimming," boy teases princess
"Swim with him!"

—Cupid, your thighs do play Cupid, boy,
She won't get far

123

If she wants thighs
Instead of high morals.
"She says you're an isolationist, Tarzan!"
Thwarted, the boy dawdles on the syllable *Tar:*
"A what! Boy?"
—Wait till he finds out!

You'll *have* to see how they do it
Tho evening prices go up quickly at noon.
"Nazi!" Tarzan says coyly
"Nazi," Tarzan says
And lures some celluloid to the lion's maw:
And all the earth's problems are solved.
You have seen
A rain of dried peas does not stick to a screen,
A non-stop reflector,
(Not the black sheet of a bed),
But an heroic
Which excretes and laughs.

4

These are not my sentiments,
Only sometimes does one feel that intimate.

God, LL.D.,

I want to resign
You can have what's mine
And what ain't mine,

I want to resign
What's mine ain't mine
What ain't mine is
Thine,

SOS

P.S. I *want* to resign.

5

Wire home:

It is always
Christmas
From the air
At night;

"So, He
    really
Lived?"

6

An ornament of sentiment

He's a bit of red and gray—maybe green—rock
He's Pierrot the clown of Montauk.

He has no eyes, he don't talk—
He's Pierrot the clown of Montauk:

His cool existence admonishes
The cool yet bloody of the fishes.

Present him and walk down the beach—
He has no human tendency to squawk,
But! He's Pierrot the clown of Montauk.

Declaim his species like the clock:
Pierrot, Pierrot, Pierrot, PIERROT!—
He's Pierrot the clown of Montauk.

7

With a passion for a baby,
An age

Of zipper and plane.
The sun zips clouds, and
The wind's right back
And it won't rain!

Zip, zip, zip,
Eat quick, slo–o–ow.
The plane lands
And we meet:
The bull–itical guard, a–gain!

8

See:
My nose feels better in the air.

9

I was walking in the park
And a man came along
With his two tow-headed kids—
Boys: one 2, the other 3.
They may have been twins
They were so gentle together.
And he held out a small box camera:
"Mister, will you take our picture?"
I stopped. "Sorry,
But I don't know how,
If I did I would, gladly."
I believe they had been DP's in Germany.
"Well, look," the man said,
"You can see ourselves in the lens,
Then just press this down.
Wait! the sun must be behind."
He placed the kids
On either side of him:
Small, blue—papa, brown—small, blue.
Blue and brown showed in the lens,
The sun caught them in sky and clouds.
It was easier to
Handle his contraption
Than a song.

"The man took our picture, papa?"
"Yes, because we looked nice."
"Good-by." "Good-by." "Good-by."
. . . and good luck.
I have one print here.

10

A round

Isn't this a lovely field
    In winter?

11

Who in snow
Has lain
Does not complain.

Whittle—
Whittle—
Wee Willie.

12

R.A.E.

Chance broke the jaw of this man
For no will could have done so
            To him.

Let him dead find such repose
That will dull the days
He is not in the sun—
Our ills and our plaints.

13

Why *daylight* saving?
At four in the morning, sun takes time
    to come up—under the horizon.

But once up
It's the sun.

Four hours sleep would be plenty
If today were enough to get up for
    and make coffee.

14

It never pours, it draws
On St. Valentine's—
An ocean
Secret with mines.

Magnetic hearts—
Moving shoeshines—
In the lines of force
Of St. Valentine's.

15

I'm a mosquito
May I bite your big toe?

    Here's ten dollars

Use it
    as you know.

I'm a fish
And I dance in your dish.

    Here's ten dollars

Go and
    say Hello, Hello,

You're Hey!

Happy
    is
       music!

The flute
The flute
The fluke

MICHTAM

The lines are fallen unto me in pleasant places;
yea, I have a goodly heritage. Ps. 16

1

Lese-Wiat, from Caul Gate

Caul Gate, Farewell, that hath me bound
And with an ointment laved my teethe
Until mine own voice tired, the sound
A quiet wasting summer's breath

Babylon his flood is stilled
Babel her tower doeth tie my tongue
In the willow path there it hath swilled
My spirit, His case, and young.

2

Romantic Portrait

Broad-bottomed Sealea
Whose potatoes are mealy—
Starched willy-nilly
His bosom grows hilly;

Whose head was cloudlike
Has become dowdlike:
His lips loose
Enough to suggest
The slack tongues
Of his shoes.

With a capital P

To the Gentlemen of the Press
With a capital P
A plea that in what sodden state he be
He will not veer nor keep his head on he

Attend him Star!
Especially in his motorcar.

XENOPHANES

Water, cold, and sweet, and pure
And yellow loaves are near at hand,
Wine that makes a rosy hand
Fire in winter, the little pulse.

Eating a little pulse, who are you?
How old? The hands of all are clean.
Why first pour wine into the cup?
Water first and the wine above.

Better than the strength of horses,
I come back to my other words:
The hound, "Stop beating him, I said,
I knew him when I heard his voice."

For now the floor and cups are clean,
The aired earth at the feet is seen,
The rainbow, violet, red, pale green,
Men making merry should first hymn—

NON TI FIDAR

in opera poetry must be the obedient daughter
of music

Mozart

The hand a shade of moonlight on the pillow
And that a shadowed white would seem above or below
Their heads ear to ear, hearing water
Not like the word, the flickflack of the eye opening on it
With what happiness
Where the word is the obedient daughter of music
And Don Giovanni's shapely seat and heart live in hell
Lovable as its fire
As all loves that breathe and kiss
Simply by life
Rocking to sleep and flame:
So frail is judgment
It must light up, an overseer
With some truckling in hell,
A song that lovers' heads
Ear to, and on ear foretell.

CHLORIDE OF LIME AND CHARCOAL

I

1 There when the water was not potable
   Because of too many microbes
   The health officer proposed
   Hanging a bag
   With a mixture of chloride of lime and charcoal
   Ten feet down in,
   To purify the well.

2 Zinnias you look so much like Gentiles
   Born among butcher furniture
   Who lived Easter and Christmas
   Whose fathers died without wills
   And left land to divide
        among they forget
   Which spinsters and

The son a saint they must have called him
        soft in the head
To whose salt marsh—it happens I like
        cattails—Jewish I am mortgaged.

Almost prize flowers, large—
I am taken aback by a difference
As by his small wife's girth
While the rest of her sweetness suffers arthritis
Whom I greet in the way
My own wife hurried to arrange you in our coffee pot
The first vase at hand
A something to give
One whose cares should be
A velvet painting of zinnias
But not her sons running off
        she might think not to learn.

As your rose, pink, yellow, and orange
Are mixed in the melting pot
That the kindness of our mortgagers
Created with you at leaving you at our door
And tho your givers begin to shake hands with my kind
Do the snobs, salvagers of culture and religion dare suspect
We are saved, formally, by green?

So: these are your lancet leaves, tubular stems
Stopped in the lotus or artichoke of your sepals
Of Egypt.

3 How sweet is the sun, is the sun
   How sweet is the sun
   With the birds, with the summer months
                the notes of a run
   How sweet, sweet is the sun.

   You ask what I can do—
   My name is Jackie

I am Jack-of-all-trades:
Homer—the carpenter—
Did you write that book?
Is your fir squared
        and its end true?

How sweet is the sun, is the sun
How sweet is the sun
With the birds, with the summer months
        the notes of a run
How sweet, sweet is the sun.

II

Homer's Argos hearing
Handel's Largo as
The car goes

Or

The dog in the third story
Brownstone window looks
Down into the street
Left and right
Much like his master
Distracted,
To see
What is going
On in the world.

Is the skyline still there
Are the buildings
A new bridge
Or the new ramp?
Philosophy moves
Faster than sound
To what purpose?

Until lights hang—
As if—from the skyscrapers—
Down a mist?

Indian summer, november first,
Evening of cantilevers of finance
Death (is?) the common share
Of the loved.

Stone struck
By hanging jewels
And hung off iron.

Are they coming home, master?

III

W

Ah, my craft, it is as Homer says:
"A soothsayer, a doctor, a singer
and a craftsman is sure of welcome
where he goes." Never
have I seen anything like you,
man or woman.
                    I wonder looking at you.
Well, in Delos
once I saw something like you,
a young palm sprung at Apollo's altar,
I've been even that far—along
with others and their raft of trouble.
Seeing that sapling I was stunned
for no other tree like it grows out of the earth.
And yet I wonder and am stunned—
you might be that girl—
at the thought of touching your knees.

READING AND TALKING

Cauliflower-eared Spartan
Who go about
Your cestus bound to the hand
What are you hiding
The cestus girdle
Of Aphrodite

That sends love on the wind
Has not lifted?
What is the hurdle—
That you rule the world
By such wisdom?

And Plato said, not
Much better
Than a few things:
'Nor when love
Is disinterested
Is there any disgrace
In being deceived.
All creation into being
Is poetry or making.
But that
Made with music
Is named poetry
The same holds
Of love, only desire
Of good
Is the fire and light
Power of love.

They drawn towards
Love by the path of money-making,
Gymnastics, or philosophy,
Are not named lovers.
The simple truth is
That men love the good.

Would you like
The truth about love
In any order
That comes
Into my mind
At the time?'

Make music, Socrates,
The dream bids
Like the runner
Bid by eyes that see:

To run as he is
Already running.

And Plato forgot to keep still
Building
A so-called good-for-all
With a cestus.

But I take it
    Too
He said—
Talk is a form of love
Let us talk.

The voice that first startled
    bodies
After they fail continues
To startle minds with abstractions
That hearts may pound again—
To a grammar
Aping a carved throw stick
Reindeer horn,
Tusks,
Lines, graves of lions,
The blood of old cave drawing

With new artifacts
Startling
A modern cave

      (Present?)

As a coda begins—
    A simple—

  That year's
  poem
  will be
  better

  if tears
  show him

to the
letter.

"AS TO HOW MUCH"

Of the right way
That branches may be
Described—
Laden with snow—
What proscribed
A limit long ago?

We do not know
Of any we see—
Inscribed
Here bark is next snow.
Love is so. Thrived.
And we do not know. No.

As to how much
Such love may be
Ascribed
To bark or snow
You proscribed
Some music long ago.

GEORGE WASHINGTON

Is it possible
Some Virginian
Laughing in
Snow's gust
Eye on beast, covert
At land
So virgin
Saw there
A father
Who could not lie.

Framed him and goat:
Who would not lie,

Nor wood, a cherry—
And chopped the
Tree down:
So people
Make blue sky,
Wig and dust white,
And covert cloth
For the first
In the hearts of—

Chopped the
Cherry tree
Down—
And chopped—
It is possible.

AND WITHOUT

And without
Spring it is spring why
Is it death here grass somewhere
As dead as lonely walks
As living has less thought that is
The spring.

Spring it is spring why
Is it death grass somewhere
As dead as walks
As living has less thought that is
A spring. And without.

PERCH LESS

Perch less, bird
Fly on the
Leaves
Be heard
Spatter drops
So nothing is
But light

So light so well
Foolishness is joy.

Butt age, boy
Have it not tell
You, *swift but*
Is nothing so
Light it drops—
From such high
Slurred notes
Bow-hair dares bird:
So light so well
Foolishness is joy.

AIR

How my city has grown!
Privet close at the window,
We have seen
New stone at the old thrown down,

Springs coiled; iron rib, spade
The excavation for the tunnel
Over which
The approaches meet at grade.

For all their metal we are not alone—
Hedge and human
As it were sun winds met on Sunday
High up and in a street of stone.

This Egypt, a downtown never to go
But, under bridge a river, to harbor
With a thought
Of ashlar to arbor.

My father praying at my mother's grave
Heard his father's song
Love and book
Not their dust where we don't pray.

We are so much alive, child, were
All his city's old graves to go
Out of sight, its harbor
Would carry his old air.

PAMPHYLIAN

Whole night in form the whorl on earth
Of Er Pamphylian by birth
Whom Plato broad forehead and throat
Held as eight sirens hymned one note.

Chains of heaven let down their waves
Three voices sound here one tone craves.
These? The daughters', of necessity.
But this thing then that has plenty

Understands together fails not
Of future nor frees its past thought
And so mighty that all be right
To touch in the middle of light

Pleasance and presence of trace
A feathering moving a face
Who are mine having nothing to save
For your grace such it cannot but have.

TO MY VALENTINES

From one to two
is one step up
and one and two
spell three
and we agree
three is the sum
                a run
of two and one.

ON VALENTINE'S DAY
TO
FRIENDS

The hearts I lift out of snow
  So few,
The one, two or three, say few
  Friends who
Eye a heart, wish well what
  I do,
Befriend its festival
  When to
Persist I sing of Celia and
  Of Paul
To R'lene and Edward, Lorine,
  Or all—
Tags, René—that can with a red heart,
  Valentine,
Brush a white-velvet heart in snow
  falling deep to speak
   Be mine.

ALBA (1952)

In sleep where all that's past goes on—
A dawn loves more than sleep.
Clear as leaves of spring.

Loves no less, wintering,
Greener than summer goes—
A sleep gainsays the dawn.

OLD

  'More do I love cold
  than do I hate warm.'
  If what the child hear
  sound old, neither does

cold hate warm.
The more if less love
may do hate out
of its charm.

SPOOK'S SABBATH, FIVE BOWINGS

I

spiccato

There was the mechanicalism
of the ice cream scooper,
the Malayan violinist
more expressive than any Caucasian
as he melted into his Schumann
so for his part hard objects
became the buttocks of the heart.

II

martelé

No sins or
Faux pas
Disturb a *repas*
À l'hôtel
The
Hotel Windsor.

Day begins or
Ends
The knee bends
To the rustle
Of cards
At the Windsor.

Never a fiesta—
A siesta
Has emptied
All the chairs

Of sins or
Faux pas
At the Windsor.

III

grand détaché

The night
the skunk
stank up
Adirondack
"the village beautiful"
Celia dreamt
of renting
outhouses
under
compunction
and beneath
contempt
while Louis
with usual
curiosity
as to *real*
estate
hung round
to look into
all, and
at last
two
to see
which
was
the better
for the
violinists'
trills
above
around
about—
brooked by
an inexorable Teacher

swayed
to the
Rode.

IV

collé

When *The Mill*
the artists colony
burnt down
we rushed
to its
end of town
to ask
"How did it happen?
Was anybody hurt?"
"No, the tank blew up
on my competitor—
my best friend—
there was no stopcock
and in this heat the oil—"
(sculptors had saved some
underwear
upon the pines)
said George, fifteen,
with teeth,
crew cut black hair,
in his "father's truck"—
stopping on a rival
call.

V

staccato

Said Susan, dear Susan
"I could faint
But I'll paint,
My relations
Who bought a cottáge here

Are all
Drinking potage."

Then Eva the diva
Sang over-all, ah
What is
The matter?
Poor good people yet so strange
I would say
With Shakespeare
They make *mows*
For *hellos*. Not so?
An effervesence makes them retreat,
Hello, a mew, never stop, go—
They pass out
On the street
I travel everywhere,
Italy—I make friends
With whole villages
All are happy, all live,
Live!
I live here too
Never mind,
I sing, I eat, I dress
And grow fatter.

"ALL WISE"

Footprint and eye fringe
Shake off snow—
All wise
Flinging.

Pupil and fingers
Draw the bow—
All wise
Singing.

Heartbeat and feathers
Sow birds so—
All wise
Ringing.

FOR
SELMA GUBIN'S
UMBRELLAS

Reality is and is
not commonage,
painting
is paint—

three headless
coats under
three
umbrellas

two yellow
and one blue,
a play as on
nightshade or eggplant,

worn like each coat
to open differently
on tubby figures
walking in shoes

red hands
around red handles
the red
holds grasp

where those other
colors
distributed
by it

are here for
a yellow splint
T'd by a shorter
slanting

that's post
hanging

a lamp
but a small

white
circle
out of
moon

a light
umbrella-wise
a way
distributed—

seen
as when
color first
made shape

by color
dividing
joining
color

until what
period
comment
followed

rain is wet
wind hugs cold
green is a patch
snow melts

into slush
in one
age
of the street

on which
as paint

are there
or are there not

three Chinese
in one spot
who don't
meet

sunlight is
on the ground
storm is in
the sky

and an after,
before, of time
but a no time
in things

so shared
no word attacks
and never
loses.

THE JUDGE AND THE BIRD

The house was Dutch
in style
of which there is—
not much.

Corbie gable,
corbel
derived
from the raven

for the reader
of a herbal
under the high
window
of colored panes

shadowing
rainbows
on
oak floor.

The old judge
dead now
lived to bring up
his trees

was well-read
on his herbs,
and his poets
in fine bindings.

Winter's gone
spring has come
and summer's here
his son rents to us.

We breakfast
facing a mountain:

a yellow—wild!
a yellow leaf—
not fall's
the yellow leaf a thought—
is yellow bird.

Casual
the wild canary's South
shows north, songless,
yellow on
pennywort

yellow near myrtle
upon moss
next my lady's-thumb-grass.

Its song its yellow says
	that stills—
the mouth

tastes pine and raspberry
digitalis and wild rose

that the tongue which may sing
be casual—
as Dutch leaf is cheap,
a gold—

as old as the Dutch style
as such of a judge
a wild South brings yellow
today—

singing of it
in crossing the brook
he deliciously called
The Bouquet.

ALL OF DECEMBER
TOWARD NEW YEAR'S

1

Not the branches
half in shadow

But the length
of each branch

Half in shadow

As if it had snowed
on each upper half

2

A tired—much less—an old
man does not talk of justice
—much less an old man
having nothing, nothing like
content

A WORLD ATLAS in a globe base:
Who turned the print to us?
We don't need to read it.

Turn it to the toile
That hangs on the wall,
The hand-blocked figures
Such blue shades
Should read it
And come to life,
The young sun.

The young son:
"If it's turned
from us, we
are the shades."

H.T.

Being driven after the hearse thru suburbs—
   the dead man who had been good
   and by a coincidence my father-in-law,
I sped by shop signs:
   Handel, Butcher, Shelley, Plumber
a beautiful day, blue wintry sky
such is this world.

SONGS OF DEGREES

1

        With
       a Valentine
   (the 12 February)

Hear, her
Clear

Mirror,
Care
His error.
In her
Care
Is clear.

2

With a Valentine
(the 14 February)

Hear her
(Clear mirror)
Care.
His error.
In her care—
Is clear.

Hear, her
Clear
Mirror,
Care
His error.
In her,
Care
Is clear.

Hear her
Clear mirror
Care his error
In her care
Is clear

Hear
Her
Clear
Mirror
Care
His
Error in

Her
Care
Is clear

Hear
Her
Clear,
Mirror,
Care
His
Error in
Her—
Care
Is
Clear.

3

'Nor did the prophet' *

The birds are our friends—
       Jannequin's,
       The sun's.
The man is our friend?
Our friend.

I know why David moves me,
"The worst bastard of them all"
Never chartered nor coddled his ground.

The sound in the Temple built after exile
Is never worth the sound
At the earth where no temple stood
And on which no law of exile can fall.

Blood flows; not hateful good,
Not this measure is blood.
Crabbed and lovely both is root.
What is never imposes.

The tree's good of the field of Machpelah
As of Persia or of Mytilene.

Who comes as Cyrus proclaims,
Rocks later with Artaxerxes,

For all Darius gives—
Rends coat, plucks hair of his head
                and his beard
Sits down astonished

And does not stop from drinking water
As blood is shed—
Does not see morning without a cloud
Upon tender grass after rain.

On this earth
We will not—nor did the prophet much—
                    mention

David.

The birds sing:
The man is our friend,
Our friend.

* *Ezra* 1–6; *I Chr.* 6.31, 15.16; *II Sam.* 23.4; *Gen.* 23

4

Happiest February

Many more happy Valentines.
How many?
As the last
      makes no sense.
As many as many.
As more rolls out the vines
Which shade green in the snow
Of a cold fourteenth
Of their happiest February.

5

William
Carlos
Williams
    alive!

Thinking of
Billy

The kid
shoots
to
kill,

But to
the expanse
of his
mind

who heard
that word
before,

scape
of a
letter

soars
with the
rest of
the letter

gulled by
the kid's
self-sacrifice:

reach
C
a cove—
call it
Carlos:

smell W
double U

two W's,
ravine and
runnel:

these
sink
high

in
high
fog

which
as
it
lifts,

the other
world
is
there:

the sight
moves—

open—

soothes

smoothes
over

the
same word

that
may have,
to touch,

two faces—
the heart
sees into—

of one
sound:

the
kid
's torn,
shot

so quickly
it sounds
water:

purls

a
high
voice

as with
a lien
on
the sky

that becomes

low now
frankly

water—

called also—

softly—

a kill.

6

A wish

Looking down at the water
three blocks away at Clark Street

if but once a day,
       my valentines,
but day after day,
my mind going to work
with eyes on the water
tries me with a prayer,
       my sweet,
that my wish wear our look
well, care for our days:
       to long life!
So the song be for good
and that time a new's written
the water flow on,
as there now, it be a completion
to wharves below, a street
away. A way—

a good sprag memory
so the boy profits lively.
It would make sense. As if there now
that time brightens a page—
stretched as by Providence—
of a mind that
in the Latin of Parson Evans—
telling the boy the vocative
Remember, William, is 'caret'—
Shakespeare went before
to touch Bach who taught
his choir boys Latin
in the while
proved by the fugue

Look, where his master comes;
'tis a playing-day,
I see.

See I, day-playing
a 'tis;
comes master his
where,
Look.

7

March first

Remarkably all this March first
Would-be, small leaves are making a hell
                    of a noise,
Littlest children fight with their fathers,
The mothers are distracted or
                    stark mad
Rehearsing with them—
Tiniest green and teemingest teen—
        Reciting
"We are the generations of leaves."

THE GUESTS

In the mountains
the finches

are
four chairs

arranged
catty-corner

before the window
on whose sill

tomatoes ripen

from above
on the
chimney
piece
the clock

ticks
down

at the door
the lawn
rolls
to the road

lined
one side by

rock wall
the space
in it
the gate to
the garden

a side post of
goldenglow
a side post of
apple tree

the garden
for what

came
to the table

as herb
or green

or vine

a mown
tract then rolled

to the two-hundred
year pines
the brambles
the woods
the sometime dry brook

brimming for once
with

wished-for
rains

and the range's
rim rose

five thousand feet

the view
from the window

two chairs
for the occupants

two chairs
standing
for the ever-returning
guests

CLAIMS

*Ferdinand
Pericles*

a poet wrote a long story with the first name
his title, and without thought that a thought
had carried over went on to the second for
a title, certain the name made Shakespeare's song
To sing a song that old was sung, From ashes—
Antioch's. Both names it occurred to him,
glad ten years with the second, mean *risking life.*
To pronounce the first letter of the first
the lower lip's bit by the upper row
of teeth, while the upper lip furls, the breath
as if held about the palpable heart;
to announce the first letter of the second
both lips persist passing teeth and the heart's breadth.
After ten years he thought thought is that risk
whose claim claims claim, *Ferdinand* stakes *Pericles*
as the breath blown follows a breath drawn in—
as the body has the thought it will live out
as what is after begins what was about.

THE LAWS CAN SAY

for P.Z.

We may not always rate
An Idaho potato—
A satisfying meal
Holds more than broken Plato.

If undersigned
Has wonder signed
It is not *prior to,*
Neither/nor, nor *and/or*

Under the law's fedora.
The best *and/or* we sing
Who hold is always
In Andorra.

SHANG CUP

From a libation cup
of bronze
which stands

on a thought
its three feet are man—

so any pair of two
make wonder, sign

a writing of that stance
seen from all planes

as the base
cradling the cup

with half-circle
of an ancient ear
the handle—

a turtle dove
sings in jade
nests part of the lid

closed on the lip

but its beak and wings
raised to heaven

this way
the eye of it
looks up

singing
come sip
I drink.

AN INCIDENT

leaning on my left hand
holding a cigarette
too close to the ear
shocked
I heard its ashes
crackle
as if a bonfire
lit up
yesterday—
and equally
forgetful
today.

THE RECORD

Some years before we were married Celia gave me a recording of the orchestral music of *Eine kleine Nachtmusik* for a birthday present, the quartet music of which our son Paul would perform the first violin part on her birthday, Jan. 21, 1956, at a public concert celebrating the 200 anniversary of Mozart's birth 6 days later.

Our valentine the heart proposed by three,

Our vanity that talks and cannot see

As it fell out—the girl who loved brought me

The record we played for ourselves years way

Before our son bowed it on your birthday,

Against fall-out,

Never to fall out—

Delight, Amadeus, to light

The music of a little night.

Barely and widely

Barely
  and
    widely

love

they say—
    in these words—

of Paul
   "barely
      twelve"

and of me
    "widely
       published

    throughout
       a long
         career"

   So unknown

Celia
  you are the peer-
    ess of this
      song

making the news notes
sing
  as there

our music is called—
  smiling
    "Make sure

call your next book—
        Barely and
                        widely"

dear.

1

This is after all vacation. All that
matters is, all that matters—neither am
I, intent on poems, desirous of hearing
all these violin and piano sonatas
every morning for over two weeks and—
tired you would rather not—
as for the young violinist who'd gallivant
rather than work fingers for stops,
fingers for keys—
yet really not. He will say: *all that* matters.
The music comes from another time
and sings it is *so,*
by it *may we* be believed,
know fingers for keeps,
creditably conceive the changes of times
retained in different pieces of music
as a *matter* of us so *they* are believed:
Beethoven's second and fifth violin and piano
sonatas have come to the measure
of two different rooms,
two instruments affecting a third creature
so young he exists in all rooms;
from low string sounds hautboys, such
as treasure today mere oboes, and now
hunting horns, and again strings are themselves
or flutes in the higher positions,
and from piano keys,
which some fiddlers scorn,
cellos, and from
the G string—airs, airs.
All who matter have come
without effacing *ever,*

so easily said, as unlacing
what is
from what was
those who have just got up
may lead or be led back to bed
having contemplated without template to
flower so.

2

You who were made for this music
or how else does it say you,
move thru your fingers, or your bow arm, lead
to this glory: God has—God's—
but one's deepest conviction—
your art, its use—you, happy,
by rote, by heart. Is thought?
What was broken was sense
but is happy again almost seen,
the first trembling of a string a worth
whose immortal ground drops so often
you plait viable strands for your use.
Or so pride loving itself looks
to more fortunate glory, with a power
apart from the trembling sense
only glory restores.

3

The green leaf that will outlast the winter
        because sheltered in the open:
the wall, transverse, and diagonal ribs
        of the privet that pocket air
            around the leaf inside them
            and cover but with walls of wind:
it happens wind colors like glass shelter,
            as the light's aire from a vault
            which has a knob of sun.

4

A Valentine

This
is
not
more
snow
to
fall

but
a
gust
of
the
softest—
bending

down
the
wood
of
gardens'
branches
into

a
girls
and
boys
pastoral,
old

years
not
to
wink

looks,
middle

life
to
chase,
it's
musical

5

The heights

The sun's white in the high fog
that a thin mist at the eyes
shows to this harbor makes see white
and extends white with wide gray of
water as into some foreign public square—
one yacht sail, few dark screws of smoke
float a deceptively unflowing threshold
for the grayed walls on the other
shore: then like quick speech the pearled cartoon
of skyline, of windows curiously
close to pavement here, what is heights
very near under at this stage.

6

Send regards to Ida the bitch
whose hate's unforgiving,
why not send regards?
There are trees' roots, branchtops
            —as is
one who can take his own life
                and be quit
except he might hurt—as
                he imagines
here he's gone—
a person, two; if not the sun.

Stratford-on-Avon

1957

The Midlands' *a* is mostly an *i*
Said like *eye*—
"We don't fancy Shixespeare here—
People come from all over the world
To see the birthplace and the grave—
But we have a picture house we go to;
The top of the station is the way
    to Anne Hathaway's cottage at Shottery,
Mary Arden's house is at Wilmcote, 4 miles
    from Henley Street."
"You've a factory here,
Stratford's become industrial?"
"Not really, those are our gas works
    you see at the bottom."
"You need gas to cook with at that, don't
    you?"
And his remains that two Americans
    and their growing son came to see
Might be thought loving
Those works too—
Tho not so much as the mother
    guiding with her baby in the pram
The three ran across again later,
    several times,
As they strolled thru the town.

She had green eyes—
No tall perch, Helena,
Of the Bard's or Swan's
          midsummer dream,
Rather small Hermia
    with whom tall Helena pleaded,

We, Hermia
Have with our neelds created both one flower,
Both on one sampler, sitting on one cushion,
Both warbling of one song, both in one key—
   we grew together,
  a double cherry, seeming parted.
Not tall personage, rather
Hermia—who as
The course of true love never did run smooth,
Guessed love's hell is
O hell! to choose love by another's eye,
Taught *trial patience*
    a customary cross

   Until
   Theseus judged:
No doubt they rose up early to observe
    the rite of May
Good morrow, friends. Saint Valentine is past:
Begin those wood-birds but to couple now?

Maybe as do all the flowers Shakespeare
    remembered
Today planted in the garden
Back of the Birthplace

Good friend for Jesus sake forbeare
The slab might be thought to pray
    for itself
Stone in the chancel stone
Looked on by the full-blown polychrome
    bust
Which such as it is might also not seem
To fancy Shakespeare here—

Anne Hathaway's burden—

And the new Queen's,
She dedicated
A rose tree
Altogether
Too wiry to see;

Or the dark
Young man's
With the Midland *ai*
Forelock,
And a girl on his arm,
Teasing:

"The one blotch
On the Shakespeare arms
In Stratford
Is the Memorial Theatre
A woman planned"
As the family of three
Can no longer
Live by thinking
Has one smile,
"That may not be bad
If it turns out well."

8

This year
that Valentine is
late—

not that the
view
distracts,

on Washington's Birthday
the cold
is

lonely
the Flag too
over Governors Island

between the Statue
of Liberty
and

the cruiser
still
in midwater between

the copings of
two
buildings (as

an island in
itself
towards

the hills of
Staten
Island)

since
Valentine's Day—anchored
for the

Picture Post Card
of the crescent
of

his evening
and the red sky
and

the blue
and
for this once

forever,
the
white

star
that is
you.

9

Ashtray

The baited
bear
on
the ashtray

shows more
flare
than the
tramp

in his whip
tho
perhaps
enough's

there
to
give them
heart.

10

Another Ashtray

Three
crimson
mongrels
bait

the whip
in a boot
on a
leg.

11

Head Lines

A San Francisco chronicle.
The voice of the West.

Paternity: 2 men say
They want boy.

'I'm the father,'
Both men say.

Krushchev
won't debate
satellites.

12

4 Other Countries

Merry, La Belle
    antichi, tilling—
of pastime and
    good company:

Tea in England
    as much as you eat
it saves face
    the fill hole's petite—

Luggage, the
    tour complete
the buttocks
    wet—

On the way to
    Tours, the russet

cow, bordering
    the river

La Gloire in the black
    flags of the valley
of the
    Loire—

A lavender plough
    in Windermere
the French blue
    door

Of a gray
    stone
house in
    Angers

Walled farms
    little lanes
of entry, orange-
    red roofs

A period farm
    cowboy on
a live green
    rivulet

Longs
    for ranches
cultivated
    plains

A horse opera
    of Indians
to end with
    the train's past.

On the route
    to Poitiers
a garden of
    purple and red

As only the French
        can plant
in front of
        an arcade of poplars'

Arc de triomphe
        infusing all
madeleine memories
        of the Ouest.

Bedlam
        Paris
Roman
        London—

Where stop
        who have spoken to
old friends
        for the

First time
        years
sing to
        speak

There is no
        quiet in the
world—a
        wedding-

Cake Tower of
        Babel
that is
        Nice—

Nor drive
        chasing
shape
        in rock

Color
        of Lascaux

bones,
     Eyzies.

The birds of
     Périgueux
sing back Gaul
     Roman and Jew

Middle Ages slum
     merde at St. Front
pendentive
     of Istanbul

Arcades, basilicas,
     chevets, the Tower
of Vésone
     in honesty

Warning
     Stay away
the wall
     crumbles—

The
     park's
a garden
     landscaped with

A butterfly
     of flowers'
hanging spread
     on ground,

Red rose fall
     in the small
arena's ruin
     red briar

Song in
     marbles of
Bertran de Born
     and Girault de Borneil.

This hush that
    the bard
is writing
    again

The vowels
    abide
in consonants
    like

Souls
    in
bodies—
    paradise is his

Hand,
    paradise
our
    speech;

To perfect
    makes
practice,
    a ray of

Sun
    he spoke
too soon,
    as on the

Legendary
    map
the
    criminal

Dropping
    always in
monk's garb
    into the

Grot
    lower

than the
	rise

He
	first
began,
	as a hole

In a head
	St. Michael
made
	in a bishop

Sent
	to sit
for an
	eternity

To look thru
	one window
of a
	Merveille

Not with eyes
	but after
he had died
	and built

Up to the mount
	where the Druids
in white surplice
	sacrificed—

Red drops
	blinking
to the Three Kings
	rubies—

Master
	Aristotle's eternal
whiteness of
	a day.

Benedictine
    initial—
golden green
    serving

Pontorson
    with croissant
on breakfast
    gingham

A
    bottle of
liqueur
    Michelaine

A tourist
    forgot in
the gap
    of a removed stone

Under an
    arch of
a
    stairway

Of the
    Perilous
Castle,
    under

Which
    endless wind
stirring
    reflections

Of clouds
    reaches water
on an Elysium
    of sand—

Yellow,
    pearl,

shadow,
   gloss-

Black—
   in one's
youth
   old women

Begged in
   the street
all the way to
   the archangel

Saint Cecelia
   who cannot praise
them
   smiles

They have
   turned young
again in shops
   on sales

Of fake
   Quimper,
Durham's
   more solid

With Bede's tomb,
   Chartres'
two towers
   as once

Measure
   Leoninus
to
   Josquin.

Merry
   La Belle are
England
   France

Short of
      a month
of pastime
      blossoms

The wish
      that of
good company
      there be

No end
      sped around
wall
      of rock

Over
      the Middle
Sea
      to where—

He
      was at
via Marsala 12
      an era gone

Now known
      of no one
except Gino Pasterino
      an old man

Assures from
      that balcony
we looked
      down.

The noise the
      beach of parasols
obscures—
      the place

Gets no rest
      from the sea

it hides now
  　—nor eyes.

Understanding:
  　I wasn't going to say
for fear
  　You didn't want to hear.

That's the worst
  　of understanding,
a handshake
  　would be better.

And of
  　Antichi
there is
  　no end.

That song
  　is the kiss
it keeps
  　is it

The
  　unsaid worry
for what
  　should last.

By the intimacy
  　of eyes,
or its inverse—
  　restiveness

Of heart—
  　Pisa's Baptistry,
Nicollà Pisano's
  　pulpit

Cannot—*antichi*—
  　hold a candle
to light the
  　circle of rock

Sculptures
        in the shadow
of round
        wall—

Primitive
        monumental
nameless
        as the carver

Who hewed—
        constraining
his shapes
        to rocks,

A lion and Judah
        perhaps,
a king—David
        by his harp,

The mother—
        married to
his line—
        her granite

Suckling
        the child—
manifest
        as the thigh

Of the
        Triumphant God
on the mosaic
        Judgment

Seat
        that Cimabue
directed
        in the semidome

Over the apse
        of the Cathedral

across
    the close.

Beside this
    seen that
legs
    would walk to

Duccio's
    chromatic story
in Siena's
    museum

Is subtle
    only
when lighting
    from

The green hills
    and knolls
the great and
    true candle

That lifts
    his countryside
which it lights
    today,

As, again, out
    of all
profluent
    Florence

A great cow
    of rock
on
    a plinth

In the Museo
    Opera del Duomo
is,
    first, valid,

More than any
      later takes
of Giotto
      in paint

And should be
      after the
stillborn
      recent ruin, a

Chapel
      in Santa Croce
selling gilt
      red leather bags.

Fra Angelico's brother
      painted one stiff
crucifixion
      after another

One
      in each
cell
      down one

Of two rows
      on the
top floor of
      San Marco

Each
      martyr's wall
his
      torture,

His
      angelic
brother
      who kneeled and rose

For the opposite row
      of cells

breathed the
     whole Legend:

A horse
     or a baby
two crossed trees
     or a mother,

In one fresco
     the luminous
center
     a piece of bread

The Lord of His
     own Last Supper
holds to the mouth
     of its inseparable Guest,

All who eat there
     inseparable.
For one afternoon
     looking down

From San Miniato
     on the flower
structure across
     the Arno

We may miss
     the Masaccio's
no distance below
     in the Carmine,

But
     if they are
for all time
     there will

Be another time,
     as in Rome
after
     the rising abstract

Of square
     futurist
coliseum,
     the Fall

Before
     the Decline
built a
     ruin to order

And Nobody's
     priority
of holes
     to come.

After
     Church
rose on
     the Forum

And this
     dug up,
churches
     fell

They square
     the marble
faced
     oval

And after
     Henry
qualmishly
     shy

Of Chaim
     (life)
and an Adams
     he read

Himself
     Adam

(earth)
    "—Why!

Why! !
    Why! ! !—"
Because
    his blood

Chilled,
    for whom
a Jew
    and friend

Is embarrassed—
    there is
other time
    repeating

Like his neighbor
    the blind beggar
on the steps
    of Ara Coeli

Altar of Heaven
    cypresses hide stars
candles shine towards
    cypresses

The column of
    Trajan so
small
    below

The grandeur is brutal
    only in the cast
in the Victoria
    & Albert.

Rome is a low
    city of shuttered houses
with
    tawny or orange views

Its older ruins
        so gentle
they disappear,
        to have been

Like the old brick
        Roman wall
that falls lower than
        any new apartment,

And the Pantheon's dome
        if stripped of its coffers
is but the adolescence
        of a geometry

That pours steel concrete.
        Familial, travelled,
or effeminate,
        the Romans loved

To possess and please
        not size so much as small
marbles of Greek gods,
        and also their wives

Daughters and sons: unlike
        the Christians
in the catacombs
        who burying theirs

In their walls
        must have turned
in distraction
        to give joy

To one another
        in carving
good shepherds
        and their flocks

Or painting fish
        or ravens

when their hymns
    and prayers

Brought no daily
    bread—and for fear no
other speech than
    out of their wild eyes.

Tendril vine
    stem
grape
    bud
    •
Leaf flower
    the Roman work's
gentlest in
    the baths of Diocletian,

Stone skirts
    stone girl
drapes them on her
    wet and wind blown.

Farnesina
    stuccoes are
a snow's conceiving
    of white,

Four
    walls
of a room
    restoring Livia's

Villa Ad Gallinas
    carry continuous
garden, the green
    singing with birds

Where fruits shine orange.
    Stele
grow,
    mosaic

Tesserae
        animal and
abstract, each
        is animate.

In germ
        the ribbed vault
on a sarcophagus,
        also a tiny

Fan vault—
        so proportioned
as not to excite
        later doubts of lavishness.

So the unribbed
        vault at
San Vitale
        hints at the rib

But remains
        where
the eye can take in
        gold, green and blue:

The gold that shines
        in the dark
of Galla Placidia,
        the gold in the

Round vault rug of stone
        that shows its
pattern as well as the stars
        my love might want on her floor

The quiet better than crying
        peacock is immortal
she loves, knows
        it so pretty

That pretty in
        itself is enough

to love.
     She likes:

The Bell Tower
     in Venice
whose windows
     run not down

The center
     but along the side
edge; the three
     gonfalon

Poles before
     St. Mark's Basilica
like votive candles
     for the five

Kisses of the cusped
     lunettes
of the second
     story;

The bare south wall
     relieved by a tile
as tho it hung
     upon a wall at home.

Nothing is
     even,
so
     touches.

She
     came to Venice
by night
     a love that fears

Water
     and trusts the
stranger balance
     of the gondolier,

It is not a question
        with the red purple gold
of houses in water
        of a torture

Making paint stone
        or stone
wrongly
        flesh.

The Banda Municipale
        plays Boccherini's
"Menuetto"
        in the lit

Shadow of the night
        sky the roof of
the public reception hall
        of the Piazza

Ledges of
        whose palaces and church
crowd
        the pigeons asleep.

Bright to the morning
        they feed
on the swell
        of the Grand Canal

Who can drive past
        the new church of
Jesu Lavoratore,
        poor carpenter.

The faded
        fresco
in San Zeno
        of Verona,

Of the mourning
        of Jesus

down
            from the cross—

Eyes
            cannot tell
if leaves
            cover the weeping

Or if the mottles
            shred colors
where plaster flaked,
            never meant

For leaves,
            the statue
of San Zeno
            himself looks Buddhist,

And the Han-
            like carving
of the small sculptured
            squares of the bronze

Doors of San Zeno
            come much nearer
Heaven than
            Ghiberti's gates.

Of good company
            then
the screed
            is:

To Montecchio
            to eat well
for two houses
            'star-cross'd'

Or history is
            so
as the wrinkled
            signora in black

Head shawl
      says kindly
'the young from
      everywhere, as far as

America,
      come here for
Giulietta's Tomb'
      stand at

The broken lid
      (it might be
a bath)
      of the marble coffin,

A coil of
      climbing plant
comes down
      thru the grate

In the ground
      of the overhead cloister
to look
      also;

That Sunday is
      best to eat a
fruit and not
      cross the Adige

For the Roman theatre
      we see across it,
and not go
      to sit in the

Box
      of the Gens Valeria
where—a question if—
      Catullus sat?

Sirmio, almost the
      eye of islands

o Lydiae lacus
  Garda, gem,

Mine;
  this is it
which makes it
  worth it;

Three months go;
  that the innocent
pyramid of red and blue
  that suffers at the eating

Is for the movement
  of the hands to it
and the mind
  that willed to eyes;

One work of art
  to a room, the exhibit in
Milano's Sforzesco
  shows is enough;

The fresco
  or tempera
is, as of Luini,
  of green and wheat;

As on the other
  side of the Alps
the peasants
  meet Parliament;

Quiet;
  tilling;
the uplifted frozen
  wave of Pilatus;

A man
  tilling
mountain
  upland;

Liveable
        place;
whose character is
        endurable

As the eyes are moist before
        the regularly spaced
flower window boxes
        of Berne; the

Aare
        flows below, above the
old city
        old or new there's

No
        architecture
to speak of;
        walk.

Of travel's
        sickness
one's young son
        puns

Guiltless
        if world-
bred,
        'The reason

I threw up
        was not a Confucian egg
nor a Lao-tse but
        a bad egg.

How's *your* Duomo?'
        Returned to the sea
past point of no
        return

Leans over
        the deck rail—

'Not worth
        being sick for'—

It blows up
        its furtive hush
a sound that
        loses sound in

Blued white:
        'Lace.' Laundry.
'But'
        he says

'Can you
        describe it—
always
        different.'

Practice
        in lifeboat drill.
A baby in blue
        storm cape's

First to be wheeled
        off the gangplank,
the tug with something
        like a fig leaf approaches

The ship's bow.
        Go home.
There you may
        think of it.

The pyramid
        repeats
of the peaks.
        Colorado's *Red Rocks:*

The natural
        acoustics
of the amphitheatre
        between the two

Sandstone shapes
    they call
Creation
    and *Shipwreck*.

As the eyes
    near wreck
to create
    when they see

RAIL   SING   CROS   ROAD

RAIL   CROS (S)
SING   ROAD
of pastime
    and good company.

I's (pronounced eyes)

(RYOKAN'S SCROLL)

dripping
words

off

a
long
while

the
first
snow

out
off
where
blue

eyes

the
cherry
tree's
petals

HOMAGE

Homage

Of love for, to
the young—

the old's affectionate
greetings—
young greetings
multiply

a few but so
significant greetings

occasioned attentions
all outs of

their green desire

loneliness
looking to
make friends—

when all the old
much too far away
to make friends
can do

is to befriend
each single
"good"
act

and
as part of
the world's
debt

place
it or a
nuisance too
much

in eternity
as it were
of
friendship

that could be
lovable
embodiment
if some after world

offered
as

in
time:

far
out of
the world

are the
old—

so much
the
new only
young

bodies
not
backed
by back aches

show
new
only.

HER FACE THE BOOK OF—
LOVE DELIGHTS IN—PRAISES
Pericles and *Two Gentlemen*

"will you give yourself airs
from that lute of Zukofsky?"

Praises Robert Duncan

"Yes, for I would have my share"

How will his praise sound back to him?
If I let it be
To confirm
One Henry Birnbaum
        and
            quote
                him.

"I ought to thank
            Zukofsky,
a wonderful voice,
            Zukofsky."

No, my young-old well-wisher,
The second in less than six months,
That makes not you,
"That makes me eclectic"
As tho arm in arm with me
May I say your songs run up to me,
Unstring insensible judges
In their mid-century
            With their Stock
Opera House of vocables—
None of us wants to sit in it—
Not I, 55, nor you, say, forward-looking
                              back to me,
To Father Huc's tree
Of Tartary
On which we are each leaves' Poetry

Where She a breath
Comes out of drudgery
Notes a worked out knee deck her daisies
And apropos of nothing
'There are words that rhyme but
are never used together
You would never use *lute* with *boot*'—
So she has used them.

            Or again—
As where cheek touches forehead,
                        of face
      My father's *boot*
      by a *lute*
                  with eight courses—
                  I have rhymed
                  it:

To her face. Love delights, the book of praises.

HILL

Black waters'
November
clouds
high afternoon
reflections
fold, draw up
wrinkle and
web
currents
to white the
plate steel
cruiser
run in
black calm
against
a raised white
swathe
as tho for day
the Milky Way
fell
around familiar
island

hill,
autumn's mountain

1959 VALENTINE

The more that—
    who? the world
seeks me so
    to speak

the more
    will I
seek
    you.

MOTET

General Martinet Gem Coughed A-hem, and A- hem, and A-hem De-ploying the nerves of his men Right, and about face, to his phlegm. Their whangs marched up to the sky, His eyes telescoped in his head A pillow that as pillar of Eur-ope He flung to his rupture A-head.

WORDS: L.Z.
MUSIC: C.Z.

212

WIRE

Wire cage flues
          on
the roofs:

Paper   ash—whole
          sheets
in gusts—

Flawed by winds
          fly
like doves

JAUNT

1

Verona, Ohio
right 3 miles
highway is past
alfalfa

plain of corn
wheat, clover, rye,
slips of—

younglings of
peach, pear, apple,

weeping willows
hang down only
to bring up
maid Barbary's song

all at one side
all on a wall
orange
day lilies

pore as tho over
red—

evening

after their kind

alpha and omega

a first sight
of seven palomino
horses
white tails
out of their cream
bodies
almost sweeping
the ground

and as if
these are
human haunches
of an Eastern world

vines
bind the
landscape with who
named it Verona

after one
first trip to Europe
perhaps
reading
Two Gentlemen

Proteus and Valentine
or about the still
younger lovers
from fatal loins

male and female

imagining
one night

foreign farmer
or native teacher

2

The cow scraped by
the hood of the car
leaped its frightened
dung its avatar
that gentle
(not the hood)
the ungentle
driver
escaped.

3

49 states
filly
rearing on
the wind
3 ways

a little housewife
the lacy love

4

Rune

ruinin'
runs

Mexico

5

Physical
geography

a sea of cotton or
a fluff of icebergs or
waterfalls, trees, gigantic
mushroomed ivories
Chinese of whatever animal, or
huge herbs soar trunkless
banana trees

      white

illusion it is slow
the aircraft humming
at 330 miles an hour
is 5 minutes passing
a plot of plan, delta, gulf
two glints of ships
over 20,000 feet below
or just as soon
there is no
earth, God's people
are below the clouds, His
sun above, the plane
banks over virtually
a field of Arctic snow
that with the rainbow to spare
skyscape promises better than landscape.

PERI POIETIKES

What about measure, I learnt:
Look in your own ear and read.
Nor wrest knowledge
        in no end of books.
Pyrrhic nor *Pirke* do.
Mind, don't run to mind
boys' Greeks' metres gnome,
rummage in tee tomes, tee-tums,
        tum-tees.
Forget terms.
No count is sure,
more safe, more stressed,

more heard, or herds peace more
in world where hearing
is a going out
or instance up or down;
from in, different instance out.
Trust: to lip words
briefs what great (?) discourse well.

I'S (PRONOUNCED *EYES*)

Hi, Kuh,

those
gold'n bees
are I's,

eyes,

skyscrapers.

*

Red azaleas
make this
synagogue
Not the
other way
round.

*

Fiddler Age Nine
(with brief-and violin-case)

Sir Attaché Détaché.

*

HARBOR

The winds
agitating

the
waters.

*

FOR

Four tubas
or
two-by-four's.

*

Angelo

the Superintendent's
Porto Rican Helper—

See
I work
alread' start roof pla'form
ñ scratching floor
on
Eight

if
I
can do
you
good.

*

SEVEN DAYS A WEEK

A
good man
when everybody
is draping
the flag on a holiday
he's behind a box

or stamp or information
window in the
Post Office.

TREE—SEE?

—I see
    by
        your tree

—What
    do you
         see

*

A SEA

the
foam
claws

cloys
close

*

A B C

He has wit—
but who has more—

who looks
some way more

withal

than
one eye

weeps, his voice

*

AZURE

Azure
as ever
adz aver

TO FRIENDS, FOR GOOD HEALTH

(Sneezing on it:)

And the
   best

To
 you
  too

After I's

DARUMA

Daruma
found object
that is art

for good luck

    Peter's sen
    Ami
    Ren
Will:

a bit
of rock

air
fire
water
sun

slow
ember

when a
butterfly

became
his wings

aye

knew he'd have

to go
to you

seven (?)
years ago

wearing
the
jacket

I'm
wearing
here

Hear?

THE OLD POET MOVES TO A NEW APARTMENT 14 TIMES

The old poet
moves
to a new apartment
14 times

1

"The old radical"
or surd—

2

I's (*pronounced eyes*)
the title of his last

followed by *After I's.*
"After"—*later* or
chasing?

3

All the questions are answered with their own words
intellect the way of a body a degree "before"
soughed into them

if the words say silence suffers less
they suffer silence
or the toy of a paradox

a worth less worth
than that *shall* will be said
as it is

4

Aleatorical indeterminate

to be lucky and free and original
we might well be afraid to think
we know beforehand exactly
what we're doing

rather let it happen

but the 'illogical' anticipation,

music, has always been explicit
as silence and sound have

in the question
how long is a rest to rest.

In the 'old' metered poetry
the Augustan proud of himself
jingle poet as he says it

freedom also happens
tho a tradition precounts

but someone before him
is counting for him
unless it happens

that the instant has him
completely absorbed in that someone:
a voice not a meter

but sometime a meter's a voice.

5

After all—
nothing
interests me
when it is full of being.

Ground,
what there's a little sun on.

Why any nuisance
to black it out?

6

Anger, an impetuousness of kicking
the four strings off the fingerboard,
blind led the bees.

7

Now a tray—
Achilles shield
great copper boiler end

from the furnace
in the home of her ma

stands burnished
at the door—
in the disguised center hole

(where the pipe support went thru)
made one with it

3 toy translucent
plastic horses
with Greek bangs

      but 3
Red behind Black
      and
favorite Yellow Sun between.

8

Tiny sarah golden
so taken in

by the beauties
of the suites
wondrously

assumed
her friends' new
apartment

had fabulously
called in
an interior decorator.

She did not presume *they*
knew nothing of decor

tho her loves
could they tell her so
had never aspired
to a decorator.

9

Back then
on Willow Street
"Happy," that is Pat

Pat
not for Patricia

*(Shall we not see
these daughters
and these sisters)*

Patrick, rickle
old man
collected garbage

singing
and no sooner
clean

than they dumped
it on him
again

in an incinerator
for which *they* paid
rent

it was his

whence this singing
ai ai ai ai

and carrying up
broken cartons
so they moved
with their books

as the brat
fourteen
the floor
below

wailed to her
banjo
and danced the twist.

10

A roof—
turned back on water

in sun holding objects
in sunny distance—

looked into sun
warmed the closed eyelids by it,
returned round to water
opened them on a blue
of water shadow of sky

when the street below
crowded with were they neighbors that *had*
lived there—as in a newspaper neared
human ashes icy roads
Auschwitz crematories'
scattering them from a cart
pulled by twenty children
and Angel Head Doctor whipping them
Head Death cycled along

was was whistling Mozart—

to La Paz, Bolivia
that Peace
where students shouted
in the court of a hospital to
a doctor on call—
treating victims,
"*Their* names,
give us *Their* names,"
were shouted at from inside:
"They're poor people
we cannot identify them
they do not have documents."

The roof—
mountain fallen molehill

had so much to do with so little
perhaps some syllables
'head lost
why cry "bald" '?

—that to move
helped necessity.

11

When the walls
are dismantled
realize
the horror
of dust

but also
where a curtain
kept the dust from
the walls,
a white

that with most
things packed shows how
little one needs
waiting for the movers

to come.

12

Who may not anymore
show his writing to friends
not till it's print
or his dreamed words
of trooped galaxies
a night of the day
they move in

glad some envy
stopped showing
its writing to him
art is not covetous
whose life is long

drip key and murky

so they compose
wet the ants

craft name
Friendship

rocket thrust
established in lbs.
300,000

weightlessness
about
4 hours
almost another
hour of minutes

only the top
half
of the pier
of the bridge

the top
half of
facade of
skyscraper

show from
the rise
of the lonely
street

float

the water brings me all things
the valentine of
the sweet fat friend
so heavy he cannot carry his drawers

optimism gaining among steel men.

13

If the worst comes to the best
you'll have 'em all

is it better to carry a single fiddle case?
a case with two fiddles?
a consort is better?
it is perhaps lighter to carry a single one
for if not in its life
in that other of playing
the case shall be no bit of the fiddle
and the fiddle not with the case.

14

She brings me all things
the caryatid of the 10th floor
holding the 11th

goes up the stair
wearing out her little fingers
cleaning

and no one says
the pity of it

the water bringing all of the continents,
the oceans
otherwise towards the windows

have we a terrace?
when the
sun comes in
it is the
Southeast

ATQUE IN PERPETUUM A.W.

Alias to a wand the height lowered
sleep well who woke every half hour
on the hour with last breath joked
two legs were mine walk 'Glad to
hear your voice' 'Glad to hear my
own voice.' One shot and sat on
in the universe fast but unsure. Itself
sedum has come up thru rock water
slate black twilight the sky's blue reins
white sweats in mist rains storms summer
clears stars and moon rounds. We have
not walked out of this place what
have we to collect. Each privet's ablossom
I am a son of the soil.
A coast guard cutter with four orange
lights and a search- scurrying only a
boat's government and the world's raids. Wire
fence of high terrace meshes day and
night air altered sometimes by gulls swallows
helicopters and turbojets. It used to shower
Aprils but never blew winds that way.
The scholarly string player has a theory
of his tone the old hour listens
'I don't understand a thing you're saying
but it's terribly'—sleepily—'out of tune.'
Counting sevens an ornament unto my wound.

THE

The
desire
of
towing

PRETTY

Look down out how pretty
the street's trees' evening green

with the day's with them
on globular lights no Hesperides
was has fruit more lemony
orangey cherryie honeydew melon white
like several white sports cars
turned the corner no peachier
headlights blaze in dark sides
of a row of cars
half-parked on the sidewalk
while for once nowhere here
fruits smell sing the mechanics

THE WAYS

The wakes that boats make
and after they are out of sight
the ways they have made in water:
loops, straight paths,
to do with mirror-like,
tides, the clouds the deep day blue
of the unclouded parts of the sky,
currents, gray sevens or darker shadows
against lighter in and out weaving
of mercurial vanishing eights,
or imaginably sights
instantaneously a duration and sun,
and the leaping silver
as of rain-pelted nipples
of the water itself.

AFTER READING

After reading, a song

a light snow
a had been fallen

the brown most showed
knoll trunk knot treelings' U's

The Sound marsh water

ice clump
sparkling root etc

THE TRANSLATION

Wonder
  once
whence
  mulier

woman—
  Latin
mens
  sounds

other
  sense
in
  native

homonym—
  my
love
  air—

mule-
  ier
hardly
  either—

who
  can
who
  can

know
  both
is
  short—

what
  does

Lewis and
  Short

say—
  (from)
mollior—
  we

homonym
  mulley
or
  also

spelled
  mooley
why
  not

mool*ea*
  l, e, a
why
  l, e, y

spellers—
  of
Celtic
  origin—

U.S.
  a
polled
  animal

dialect
  English
a
  cow—

in
  U.S.
a
  child's

word
  moolea
or
  polled

(*adjective*)
  hornless
q.
  v.

(positive)
  mollis

Greek
  malakós
amalós
  mōlus

(confer)
  blaychrós—
(perhaps
  Latin)

mulier
  (*mollior*
comparative)
  mollis

movable
  pliant
flexible
  supple

soft
  delicate
gentle
  mild

pleasant—
  not
bad
  for

authority—
  in
shorts
  so

many
  authorities—
you
  know

what
  authority
is—
  when

short
  each
has
  authority—

Liddell
  and
Scott—
  we

little
  and
scotfree—
  blaychrós

that
  is
weak
  feeble

(*adverb*)
  blaychrōs
slightly
  no

I
  don't

like
  that

my
  blood
can't
  endure

it—
  malakòs
leimown
  a

soft
  grassy
meadow
  amalós

light
  (slight
like
  seductive)—

but
  "a
cura
  della

moglie
  del
poeta,
  che

ha
  tratto
poesie"
  who

has
  picked
poetry
  from

239

mens—
  moglie
that
  would

be
  mulier
that
  would

be
  wife
that
  would

be
  soft—
a
  sleeping

breath
  sof-
t-
   t

FINALLY A VALENTINE

There is
a heart

has no
complaint

better a-
part

than
faint

so the
faintest

part of
it

has no
complaint—

a
part.

Index of First Lines and Titles

Born in 1904 on the Lower East Side of Manhattan, Louis Zukofsky has lived in New York City most of his life. He has taught at the University of Wisconsin, Queens College, Colgate University, San Francisco State College, the Polytechnic Institute of Brooklyn, and the University of Connecticut, Storrs.